BUILT FOR THIS

A GUIDE TO TACKLING NEW DADS' TOP 16 CONCERNS
ABOUT PREGNANCY, CHILDBIRTH & BECOMING A
FATHER

ZACH TOBIN

CONTENTS

To my incredible kids whose love, affection, and admiration drive me to be a better man and whom I treasure more than life itself.

To my loving wife, who is always by my side and whose very presence makes me stronger.

To God above who has blessed me with a family that I don't deserve.

A GIFT JUST FOR YOU

THE NEW DAD'S CHECKLIST
EVERYTHING YOU NEED TO DO BEFORE (AND
AFTER) YOUR BABY ARRIVES

- A step-by-step guide designed just for dads
- 30 essential steps to take before your baby arrives
- 14 things dads forget to do during & after delivery
- A simple format that helps you track your progress and get prepared

Visit: www.built4thisbook.com **OR** scan the QR code above

INTRODUCTION

We had just stopped at a campsite near Redwood National Park on our road trip to San Francisco, and I was taking our sleeping bags out of the car to put them in our tent.

"Hon, I have some exciting news," my wife announced.

She paused. "I think I'm pregnant!"

We were surrounded by the tranquil sounds of nature, but it was like a hand grenade had gone off in my head.

While we had discussed having kids months before and agreed that we were ready to start a family, I needed a minute to process. Still, I had to say something. But, the best I could manage was an unconvincing, "Oh, wow!"

After an understandable look of disappointment from my wife and a few awkward questions on my part, we let the topic drop, and I went to get some firewood.

The irony was that I've always known I wanted to be a dad. So why did the news of a baby suddenly feel so overwhelming, so surprising, so soon?!

It took a while for me to unpack what was going on.

Yeah, we had talked about having kids, but parts of my life were still speeding down the highway in a different direction, and it felt like somebody had pulled the parking brake. I'd arrived at fatherhood.

You see, I'd just landed my dream job as an intelligence officer working for the government. It was a once-in-a-lifetime opportunity that I'd been working toward for three years, and something in my gut told me this would change everything.

I couldn't have told you this at the time, but I was concerned that I'd have to shelve my career plans, which would've involved lengthy deployments to warzones and long nights at the office. Beyond that, how would we ever save enough money for a deposit to buy a home, while dealing with all the extra costs of a kid? And, of course, our romantic plans to see the world together would have to be placed on hold, right?

I was excited to become a dad, but I still felt disoriented. I wasn't as prepared for fatherhood as I thought. Then, in an instant, everything became real when I heard those four little words: "I think I'm pregnant."

We've Never Done Anything Like This

Becoming a dad is one of the biggest changes that most of us will ever experience in life. Knowing how high the stakes are makes it all the more terrifying, even when we're excited about it.

Hopefully, you responded to your partner's news better than I did, but I'm sure you still have your own fears and apprehensions about what's coming your way. Most men do, even if it's considered taboo to talk about them.

Nobody wants his social life, hobbies, and freedom to live life on his own terms to take what seems like an indefinite backseat. Nor do we look forward to unending streams of dirty diapers, incessant noise, and sleepless nights.

Of course, those are just annoyances. At some point, we realize that our finances are about to be wrecked by medical bills and all the other costs of having a kid. And, eventually, we reach the point of wondering how we're ever going to make ends meet on a single income and still make time to be involved dads.

On top of all that, if you do have any time left over to spend with your partner, at what point will her libido shut down? Is it when that sexy playmate of yours swaps her lingerie for nursing bras and your six-pack becomes a keg?

Oh, and what about that unspoken, nagging feeling of utter helplessness that comes from knowing there's a risk of health complications for our loved ones... and there's nothing we can do to protect them?

And, even if the delivery does go smoothly, how do we know whether we're going to be any good at taking care of a baby? If you're anything like I was, you're way out of your depth dealing with newborns, and you know it.

But, for some men, the most terrifying thought of all is that we might repeat the mistakes that our own fathers made. Or, maybe our fathers were wonderful men, but we don't feel 'ready' to be dads and think we'll fail to be the dads our kids deserve.

What You're Going to Learn

In the pages that follow, I'm going to give you clear-eyed thinking from my own real-world experience to put these fears and others into perspective. Some of them are exaggerated. Others are valid. In each case,

PART I

INCOMPETENCE

Don't Over-Think What's Being Asked of You

Your job isn't to be your partner's birthing coach, suggesting all the best birth positions or guiding her through breathing techniques. Yes, gentle reminders about things you both learned in birthing class might be helpful if your partner has forgotten them in the moment, but chances are that her intuition about how to birth a baby will far exceed anything you or I will ever learn.

You're also not there to alleviate stress by cracking nervous jokes. Nobody's jokes are funny when you're squeezing an 8-pound object through your genitalia.

And you're not there to take control of the situation or try to 'fix' her pain. As hard as it can be to watch someone you love experience pain, she was made for this, and she's the only one who can do it.

As the most trusted person in your partner's life, your job is simply this: be present with her during what may be the scariest (and happiest) moment she will have ever experienced up to that point.

The October 1949 issue of *Esquire* published an article entitled "A Man's Crusade for Easy Birth: A Husband's Place is Not in the Waiting Room", which was written by a forward-thinking dad, who said it exceptionally well: "A man doesn't need to be a miracle worker to play his role to perfection [...] He merely needs to be there, period. Instead of wearing out the carpet of the lounge on the floor, he is simply required to pull up a chair to his wife's bedside."[5]

If you make a point of being physically, mentally, and emotionally present for your partner without distraction, being an active participant will follow from there. You already know her better than anybody else, and you'll be able to naturally intuit what she needs.

In the Delivery Room: Four Roles for Dads to Play

When I say dads should be 'actively' involved in delivery, I'm talking about more than the patronizing insinuation that dads are only there to be their partners' personal assistants. There's much more to our job than filling out paperwork, getting her ice chips, snapping some pictures, and making phone calls to the family—as important as those things may be.

Having been part of all four of our kids' deliveries, I'd say there are at least four vital roles that dads are particularly well-suited to play during delivery: encourager, enforcer, joint decision-maker, and masseuse.

Role #1: Encourager

The findings of a 1962 study by Dr. Robert Bradley suggest that a father's presence in the delivery room helps a laboring woman relax, which, in turn, helps labor progress.[6] That is the importance of your role as an encourager.

You may not be the first person your partner looks to for birthing and breathing techniques, but yours will be the first hand she reaches for when she's scared or in pain.

As the person in the room she's closest to, your emotional support and words of encouragement will mean more than you know. Validate her. Tell her that you're proud of her. Tell her what a great job she's doing. And, if she snaps back at you in her discomfort, take it with a grain of salt.

Also, a big part of encouraging your partner is to make sure that what you say comes from a place of genuine support and affirmation.

My wife has a friend who was intent on giving birth naturally. In the middle of labor, while she was exhausted, her husband suggested she get an epidural. "No need to be a hero," he said. Sure enough, my wife's friend caved and got the epidural, but looking back, she knew she was coping fine and regretted doing so.

While her husband meant well, and his comment might have sounded like encouragement, it ultimately undermined her efforts and downplayed her real motives for wanting a natural birth... the health of their baby. Instead of affirming the plan that they had already agreed on and encouraging her through the difficulty, he tried to 'fix' her pain and ended up sabotaging her resolve at her weakest moment.

Role #2: Enforcer

Another important role for you to play is that of enforcer, by informing and reminding medical staff of you and your partner's wishes.

With our first baby, I kept waiting for the 'right' time to tell the doctors that we wanted them to delay cord clamping, but with so much going on that right time never came. If there's something particularly important to you and your partner, you need to be proactive in bringing it up.

Especially in a hospital setting, medical staff aren't going to stop and ask you about your birth plan; they're just going to follow their standard procedure, unless you tell them otherwise.

And, as new nurses come on shift, you may have to get them up to speed again because chances are good that they won't have received a read-out of what you told the nurses before them.

Depending on your doctor, you should also be prepared to handle conflict with medical staff. Some doctors can be very pushy about forcing unwanted medical interventions like C-sections on laboring moms, rather than trying to help them deliver naturally.

If you're concerned about this, you and your partner should take that into account when choosing your doctor, but even that's no guarantee that you'll end up actually delivering with the doctor of your choice. If you do end up with a pushy doctor or nurse, who isn't respecting you and your partner's wishes, don't let the power dynamic intimidate you... push back.

Believe it or not, you may also need to 'protect' the delivery room from family members.

A few years back, my sister-in-law had her first child, only to find out on the delivery day that her mother-in-law expected to be in the room with her.

My sister-in-law wasn't particularly excited about the idea, and much to her husband's credit, he's the one who told his mom "no". While there were some hurt feelings, he gave his wife the space she needed to focus on labor.

This part is going to look different for every family. Some women want to have a 'birth party', with everybody they know present. Other women are much more private.

You and your partner should have a conversation in advance about who is welcome in the room during delivery or even afterward, so you can enforce those wishes.

Role #3: Joint Decision-Maker

It's also vital for you to be there as a joint decision-maker because there's a decent chance that medical decisions will need to be made in the moment, even for low-risk pregnancies with smooth deliveries.

You're hiring a doctor or midwife to advise you because they're experts, but make your final decisions as a couple, rather than blindly following whatever they say. Why? Because the dual incentive of avoiding liability and increasing billing codes creates a very strong motivation (even if it is subconscious) for doctors to recommend unnecessary interventions that can harm health outcomes while increasing your medical bills by thousands of dollars.

If your partner is in the midst of labor, the chances are that she won't be thinking clearly due to pain or medication. Regardless, it's not fair to place on her the burden of making medical decisions by herself. Obviously, involve her as much as possible, but make sure you step up and push for decisions that are in her and your baby's best interest.

Role #4: Masseuse

Comparatively, this last role may not seem so important, but being your partner's masseuse can do a lot to alleviate her pain during childbirth.

While many doulas and midwives will be familiar with massage techniques, don't expect it from most doctors and nurses. What's more, your partner will probably be more comfortable having you massage her than somebody she doesn't know well.

Be prepared to apply counter pressure to areas like her lower back or hips as the baby descends into the birth canal. Chances are, your partner will be able to tell you exactly where she needs you to massage, but it'd be worth your time to do some Youtube research before delivery day to learn about common massage techniques that help with labor pain.

The above isn't a hard-and-fast formula for all dads to follow, just some guidelines to help you set expectations and prepare ahead of time. Being 'actively' involved in labor looks a little different for every couple, so you may not be the primary person fulfilling each of these roles for your partner.

Preparing in Advance: Practical Tips

It could be that you won't even be able to be physically present on delivery day.

Whether deployed to a war zone, incarcerated, or unable to be in the delivery room for medical reasons, there are still ways you can be mentally and emotionally present for your partner.

Present or not, don't just fade into the background if you're not the primary person for all of these roles.

Even if you are there on delivery day, your partner may look to her midwife for coaching on birth techniques, but she'll still need your hand to hold. A doula will probably have more experience handling pushy medical staff, but it's still on you to make sure that she remembers the right details and *does* enforce the birth plan. And, yes, you may implicitly trust your doctor or midwife's judgment and skill, but you and your partner will always be the best ones to make final decisions about medical interventions and changes to care.

I said that being actively involved in delivery will follow naturally if you're physically, mentally, and emotionally present for your partner—and it will—but there *are* things you can do to prepare in advance.

These are important for every dad, but they're even more important for those dads who can't be present on delivery day.

Tip #1: Talk to Your Partner

Ask your partner what she's most nervous and excited about as well as what specific ways she's hoping for you to support her.

Tip #2: Take a Birthing Class with Your Partner

It doesn't need to be months long or even something that you pay for, but knowing the basics of what your partner will go through during labor will help you support her better and keep you from feeling 'lost'. As a plus, many of these classes even cover some massage techniques to help manage pain.

Tip #3: Talk to Your Family

Discuss boundaries with your family before the delivery date so you establish expectations early about who will be welcome in the delivery room.

Tip #4: Help Develop the Birth Plan

Don't be a passive chump and put this all on your partner.

And, no, I'm not talking about choosing which songs should go on her 'birthing playlist' or deciding what type of scented candle to bring with you. I'm talking about decisions like whether or not to try for a natural birth, whether to use a hospital or birthing center and which doctor or midwife to go with. I'm also talking about whether to insist on delayed cord cutting, opt out of the Hepatitis B vaccine, or try to breastfeed as well as all the other decisions that need to be made during and after delivery.

If you don't help make the birth plan, how are you going to know what to enforce on delivery day?

Another reason it's so important for you to create a birth plan together is so you actually understand the reasons for each decision as well as their importance.

For example, if your partner is intent on natural birth, but you don't understand that epidurals tend to prolong labor, which increases the chances of having a C-section,[7] you'll probably be more inclined to respond like my wife's friend's husband: "No need to be a hero."

Not only will knowing the real reasons behind each element of the birth plan help you encourage your partner in the right ways when things get tough, but it's also vital for making informed decisions about any changes or interventions that your care provider might propose in the moment.

I'm sure other things could be added to this list, but if you take these simple steps, you'll be well-prepared when the time comes, and you'll be playing a vital role on delivery day, even if you can't be physically present.

One of the Most Meaningful Moments of Your Life

For obvious reasons, most of what I've shared has been focused on your partner and baby, but they're not the only reason you should be present and engaged as much as possible.

As a new dad, being there for yourself may be as important as being there for them. If you do a Google search, you'll find plenty of people who disagree with me. They'll offer any number of excuses as to why dads have no place in the delivery room, ranging from getting in the way and fainting, to claims that dads slow down labor, to fears that men will lose sexual interest in their partner afterward.

While I'm sure that every one of these things has happened to somebody somewhere, they're the exception... not the norm.

The reality is that neither my wife nor I know of any dads who regret being part of their children's birth or any women who regret having their partners present during labor.

Being involved in labor isn't about catering to your 'fragile male ego' either. It's about doing what's best for your family and ensuring you don't miss one of the most meaningful moments of your family's life.

Your partner will be carrying your baby inside of her for nine months. She'll feel the kicks and punches, know whether he's awake or asleep, and internalize the fact that every decision she makes impacts him. They'll likely have an unbreakable bond before they've ever even seen each other.

Because we men don't have those constant reminders, fatherhood can seem distant during pregnancy, and it's easy for us to 'fall behind' our partners when internalizing our new role.

I think that being by your partner's side during labor, witnessing your baby's birth, and holding him during his first moments of life outside the womb makes fatherhood 'real' for a lot of dads.

That was certainly my experience. My wife says that one of her favorite memories from our first child's birth was witnessing my sudden transformation when I held our son.

While I had identified with my role of 'dad' during the pregnancy, it was no longer just intellectual as I cradled him in my arms for the first time. Much to my wife's surprise, I was even more exuberant about his birth than she was!

2

CARING FOR A BABY – IT TAKES PRACTICE, NOT INSTINCT

I grew up on a cattle farm in Virginia. There was a lot of work to be done, and my brothers and I were expected to pitch in.

During the summers, when most kids were going to the pool, playing Nintendo, and attending summer camp, we were busy clearing fence rows and making hay.

I think I was seven when my parents taught me how to drive the tractor so I could help. After showing me how to start and stop, they sat me on it, put it in first gear, and had me steer as my dad and older brothers picked up the square bales in the field and stacked them on the wagon.

Since I was so young, I had to stand on the brake pedal, hold onto the steering wheel with both hands, and pull myself down to stop the tractor.

Looking back now, as an adult, I know that it would've been really hard for me to hurt myself or anybody else, since we were in a wide-open field and the tractor was going so slowly. My dad or brothers could've easily jumped on and helped me out if needed.

Still, the first couple times they put me on the tractor, I felt uncertain... even scared. It's not like my job was complicated, it was just a lot of responsibility for a seven-year-old, and I wasn't sure that I knew what was expected of me until I'd taken a few laps around the field, at which point I became increasingly comfortable and confident.

Twenty years later, I had a similar feeling as I loaded our firstborn into a car seat and drove home from the hospital.

Just like my seven-year-old self, it's not that the job seemed all that complex. I just didn't feel like I knew what I was doing. I felt uncertain.

You see, by anybody's standards, I was out of my depth when it came to taking care of an infant.

I'm the youngest in my family. Not just my immediate family, either. I have four brothers and 13 cousins... all of them older than me by a long shot.

That means I never had any younger siblings or cousins to take care of while growing up. I wasn't around babies as a kid, and even into my teen years, they annoyed me in the few instances where I was around them.

Before our first son was born, I had never changed a diaper. I had only ever held a baby twice, and it felt weird!

Oh, and the degree of patience required to be the parent of small children is something that has <u>never</u> come naturally to me.

How About *Paternal* Instinct?

Even if you've been around kids more than I was growing up, you may still feel like being a man is somehow a handicap when it comes to caring for infants. A lot of dads feel this way. They assume that they're just not as suited as their partners to being actively involved, until their kids get a bit older and can throw a baseball.

What if you 'break' your baby? What if you don't recognize when something is wrong? What if you just can't handle being around the shrieking and howling that inevitably comes with having a newborn in your house?

Some of this hesitancy comes from differences between how the average dad and average mom interact with their kids as well as the fact that moms have a nine-month head start on bonding with their baby. But it's certainly exacerbated by the fact that our society normally portrays dads as panicked, even terrified, by newborns—otherwise capable men rendered helpless by the most basic childcare tasks if someone with "maternal instincts" isn't there to hold their hand.

But, here's the reality. Dads can care for newborns just as well as moms.

I'll give you just one example. A lot of people think that "maternal instinct" somehow makes moms incredibly good at picking out their baby's unique cry.

Well, a recent study from the University of France says otherwise. Moms and dads can both pick out their babies' unique cries from among other babies about 90% of the time. That same study found that moms and dads are also equally *bad* at recognizing their baby's cries if they spend less than four hours per day with their child.[1]

So, what's the take away? A lot of parenting is learned - for both dads and moms - and the best form of learning is experience.

Now, this isn't to say that caring for a baby is always easy. But that's as true for your partner as it is for you.

When you start second-guessing your own skills in caring for a newborn, remember that your partner probably also feels like she's bitten off more than she can chew. Other than the ability to grow breasts and lactate, moms don't possess some unique childcare gene that dads are missing.

Changing a diaper without spraying the walls and floor, swaddling a baby firmly, and bottle-feeding can all be learned from a nurse, midwife, or another parent. And, if you want to get a head start, you can learn the basics, like how to safely hold a baby, from another experienced dad to give your confidence that extra boost.

Like I said, before I held our firstborn I could count on one hand the number of times I'd ever held a baby. I had never changed a diaper, and I had no idea how to swaddle an infant. But, with all the practice I got at the hospital while my wife recovered, I was able to give my wife a refresher course when we got home, even though she's the one who grew up with three younger sisters!

Yes, on average, new moms are likely to have more experience caring for children than new dads. After all, less than 3% of babysitters in the US are male.[2]

But that type of experience may not make as big a difference as you'd think. Babysitting a toddler is worlds apart from caring for a newborn. What's more, every baby is unique and baby care is definitely not a copy-and-paste exercise.

This is true even after you have kids. None of our four kids has the same personality, and their differences started to manifest on day one. Every kid requires you to study, experiment, and adjust to find what works.

Since a lot of these skills are learned "on the job", you may find that your partner picks them up faster than you if she happens to be the one staying home with the baby while you're working full time.

That's not an indication of your ability. You can still pick these skills up quickly, if you're intentional about it during those opportunities that you do have.

Dad's Kryptonite: Crying

Now, perhaps one of the most difficult things to deal with for any new parent—mom or dad—is crying. How much your baby cries is going to affect everything, from how much sleep you get, to how much you're able to bond with your baby, to how overwhelmed you feel as a new dad.

You must never judge your parenting ability by how much your baby cries. Makes sense, right? Well, as easy as that sounds now, you'll find that it's hard to remember when your daughter is an hour and a half into a middle-of-the-night scream fest that shows no signs of abating, but you've already done everything you can think of to console her.

Crying is hard work, and it is utterly shocking (and impressive) how much willpower and endurance these tiny, feeble, helpless creatures can exhibit during their howling sessions.

Now, there's no guarantee that you'll experience this. Most of it comes down to each baby's specific personality and health status. You simply can't tell what your baby will be like until he arrives, so prepare for most of the *known* challenges and be pleasantly surprised if your baby turns out to be easier than expected.

Take my brother-in-law and sister-in-law's first kid. She was one of the most easy-going babies I've ever met. She was healthy. She didn't need to be held all the time, and I've never heard her cry.

By contrast, our firstborn happened to be both strong-willed and colicky. He'd shriek for 30 or 40 minutes straight with us holding him and attempting to soothe him the entire time. This scenario would play out numerous times every day until his colic cleared up around nine months.

Now, understand that it's pretty normal for a healthy baby to cry for up to two hours intermittently during a 24-hour period. If you find that you're spending 3-4 hours a day soothing your newborn, he might have colic, which affects about 15% of babies.

You need to be prepared to run that emotional marathon if you happen to draw the winning ticket in the colic lottery.

Caring for a strong-willed or colicky baby is normally not a question of using the right tactics. It's more an exercise in mental endurance... especially if you're somebody who already has a short fuse, doesn't handle noise well, or is under a lot of stress in other areas of life.

And this is just as true for your partner. Studies confirm that moms and dads are equally likely to cause shaken baby syndrome when they get overwhelmed and lose it.[3]

That said, there are some tactics that can be helpful.

First and foremost, never, ever, ever pick your baby up if you have even the slightest sense that you might lose your temper, especially when you're already sleep-deprived. If you have your baby in your arms, immediately put him down in his crib and leave the room. A crying baby is better than a dead baby.

It's absolutely okay to let your baby cry until you're 100% sure your emotions are in check. You may even ask a family member to take over your shift for a few hours.

As silly as it might sound, you may also want to keep a pair of ear muffs close at hand, like the ones you would wear when mowing the lawn or using power tools. So long as you can still see your baby, in case they need anything, wearing these can help to keep them safe and you sane when they won't stop crying.

Of course, these are just tactics to keep yourself in check. After all, that's the most important priority. However, it's also important that you learn to recognize your baby's cries, read their body language, and try to address whatever is causing their discomfort in the first place.

The Importance of Empathy

As frustrating as it can be to feel completely beholden to that little noise box who won't respond to any of your efforts to console her, this is where you really need to have empathy.

Babies don't cry without a reason. They cry because they can't do anything for themselves, and you're not picking up on their other body language, so it's the only way they know how to communicate.

Have you ever been wearing shoes and had an itch on your foot that you couldn't scratch? It's almost unbearable, right?

Now imagine feeling equally helpless and irritated for every single want, need, or impulse that you have, for every moment of every day, and the only way you can get anybody to help you is to cry. Welcome to the life of an infant.

From day one, start watching your baby closely, taking note of what else is going on when she cries and what it is that ultimately helps her calm down.

What you'll notice first is that your baby's cries don't all sound the same. Once again, every baby has her own code. There isn't a magic trick to this. You'll just have to decipher what each type of cry means by trial and error and comparing notes with your partner.

You'll start to listen for the pitch, length, frequency, and intensity of her cries. Hunger, gas, tiredness, overstimulation, fright, sickness, teething, and sometimes just plain boredom will each have a unique sound. You'll quickly recognize the sad, nasal-sounding whimper, devoid of energy, that tells you your baby is sick because it'll just about tear your heart out.

You'll also learn to read her body language. For example, some babies smack their lips, put their fists in their mouths, or move their heads from side to side when they're hungry. Others squirm and pull their legs up when they're gassy and crampy. Yawning and eye-rubbing with chubby fists often mean a nap is in order.

After a few weeks of attentive observation, you'll get better at anticipating your baby's needs even *before* the crying commences.

Still, regardless of how attentive and proactive you are, there will be plenty of times as a dad when you simply don't know how to help. Since whatever caused our son's colic also caused him to throw up almost everything he ate, he was only in the 2nd percentile for weight gain by the time he was three months old!

He was dangerously underweight.

Thankfully, he's healthy now, but it took nine months for that to clear up, including lots of difficult nights and days as well as an incalculable amount of trial-and-error on our part.

As a first-time dad, you'll have those types of experiences, and they'll probably make you feel less like a capable man and more like my seven-year-old self on the tractor - gripping the steering wheel as tightly as possible and pressing down on the brakes as hard as you can, just hoping you don't screw up.

Just remember, every parent feels powerless to help their kids at some point. It's not just you, and it's not just dads. But you're more capable of caring for this little person than you think, and the comfort and confidence only come after you've taken a few laps around the field.

Taking the initiative to learn ahead of time, setting realistic expectations, and being very intentional about learning to practice empathy will get you through most of the challenges of caring for a newborn.

The relentless love and perseverance of a father will carry you the rest of the way.

3

BONDING WITH AN INFANT –
BIOLOGICALLY "BUILT FOR THIS"

When my first son was still a baby, one of the highlights of my day was the short walk from my car to my front door each afternoon when I got home from work.

Since the townhouse where we lived had a French-style front door with window panes from top to bottom, my son could sit on the floor and still see out. He knew about what time I got home, so every day he would play by the door waiting to see my car pull up.

He'd plaster himself against the glass, bursting with excitement to see me coming up the sidewalk from my car. As I opened the door, he welcomed me with as much celebration, clapping, and enthusiasm as a one-year-old could muster.

Memories like that stick with you for a lifetime. And having a bond like that with your child crystallizes just what a privilege it is to be a dad, regardless of any hard work or 'costs' you must pay.

More than Sperm Donors & Breadwinners

Many first-time dads either fear they won't be able to bond with their newborn babies or don't even recognize the importance of doing so.

Unfortunately, the same outdated cultural norms from the Victorian Era, which rigidly pigeonholed women into the roles of homemaker and mother to the exclusion of anything else, also relegated men to those of breadwinner and sperm donor.

You see, there's this implicit assumption in our society that all moms are naturally nurturing, hands-on caregivers while dads should basically just be financial providers and silent partners when it comes to actually raising their kids.

No, most people won't say it quite that explicitly, but even now, well into the 21st Century, over a quarter of Americans believe that it's more important for new babies to bond with their moms than their dads.[1] You'd think that seeing the utter destruction caused by the epidemic of fatherless households over the past few decades would've debunked that myth, but apparently not.

These opinions manifest themselves in broader society in ways that have real impacts on dads and their families. Even though dads in our generation spend significantly more time with their infants than fathers from prior generations, a great majority still feel that they play a backup role to their partners when it comes to parenting.[2]

By way of example, a study conducted by anthropologists at Oxford University found that the nature of many fathers' involvement in their children's lives was dictated more by the attitudes of healthcare workers and workplace colleagues than it was by their own intentions. Many of the participants in the study specifically remarked that the prevailing attitude in society relegated them to being 'supporters' rather than 'parents'.[3]

Still, even dads who see through these cultural stereotypes might not feel like they'll be *able* to bond with their kids, almost as if dads are somehow inherently worse at bonding with babies than moms.

While these are distinct concerns, these fears are often related to the concerns we discussed in the last chapter about how to care for a newborn.

After all, if babies just 'eat, poop, and sleep' how are you going to bond with one when you're at work for most of their waking hours (assuming you're not a stay-at-home dad), and you're not the one feeding them, even when you are home (assuming your partner nurses)?

It's a fair question under any circumstances, but even more so if you're like I was before I had kids. I'd hardly ever been around babies growing up, and I was seemingly incapable of holding one without him crying.

Yes, you will have some additional hurdles to jump as a dad, and some of the biological differences between moms and dads will give your partner a head start bonding with your kids.

But, that in no way means you're any less capable of building that relationship with your infant. In fact, you are quite literally "built for this".

It's in Your DNA

Most people don't know this, but parenthood doesn't only trigger changes in a woman's body. Your body will also undergo changes to prepare you to bond with your newborn... and I'm not talking about the dreaded 'dad bod'.

Three weeks before your baby's birth, your testosterone levels will drop by about thirty percent, which is basically your body preparing you to bond with your baby.[4]

Another important hormone for bonding is oxytocin— the 'love hormone'. Many people mistakenly assume that the 'in love' feeling it causes is exclusive to moms because birth and breastfeeding cause it to spike in their bodies. However, as you hold and play with your newborn, you will also experience a spike in oxytocin, causing you to want more contact with your kid and making you feel even more connected.

Additionally, as oxytocin levels in your body increase, your testosterone levels drop further, which means you become better at soothing your baby. Your body will also produce more prolactin. Whereas this hormone boosts milk production in women, it'll make you more playful when interacting with your baby as well as more sensitive to his cries.[5]

Without realizing it, as a new dad, you already have everything (barring breastfeeding) built into your DNA to bond with an infant. No outdated stereotype or bias changes that.

It's Going to Look Different... We're Men, not Women

I think one of the reasons why many people are under the impression that moms are better at bonding with their kids than dads is because of the mistaken assumption that 'nurturing' care is the only type of 'good' care for an infant.

Yet, kids need more than nurturing if they're ever to test their limits and mature toward independence. And, while this need becomes more prominent as they get older, it starts when they're babies.

You see, I would readily admit that your average mom is much more nurturing than your average dad. While this can vary from couple to couple, it certainly holds true between me and my wife. But, I would never contend that your average dad is worse at bonding with his kids than your average mom.

Why? Because dads still build strong bonds with their kids; they just tend to rely less on nurturing and more on play.

The differences between how you and your partner interact with your baby will show up in the way they respond to each of you as early as eight weeks old. Seeing you is likely to get your baby excited, knowing something fun is about to happen, while he'll visibly calm at the sight of your partner.

A study from Boston Children's Hospital demonstrated this. It found that infants' pulse and breathing slowed and their shoulders relaxed when approached by their mothers, but their pulse and breathing quickened while their shoulders hunched and their eyes widened when their dads approached them, almost like they were anticipating action.[6]

A lot of dads will confirm this, too, acknowledging that they have more playful relationships with their kids than their partners do, but it takes them a bit longer to feel at ease as nurturers. [7]

Because of these differences in how you and your partner bond with kids, it's not uncommon for them to gravitate toward one parent over another at various times.

It's intuitive that a newborn might want mom more often than dad, since babies need to eat so often and nursing is one of the ways they soothe themselves. Yet, as your kid becomes more mobile and adventurous, it's likely that he'll be more interested in having you throw him in the air and play superman.

Don't take these preferences as any indication that you have a weak bond with your kid or let it impact how much time you spend with him. During their first year of life, each of our kids has demonstrated, in varying degrees, a preference for my wife over me. They wouldn't reject me completely, but they would often do things like reach for mom after just a few minutes of me holding them.

Then, somewhere between their first and second birthdays, I became a celebrity for no apparent reason and mom took a back seat temporarily. Whenever I would walk in the room, I'd be met with applause and cheers of celebration. Such a time to be alive!

We've both had a strong bond with each of our kids from day one, but their preferences continue to change over time.

Moms and dads don't just differ in *how* they bond with their kids, either. They also tend to differ in *when* they bond with their newborns. Generally, moms have already bonded to a great degree before they ever 'meet' their newborn because they feel his every move and think about his wellbeing every moment for nine months before he's born.

You obviously won't have that experience, so childbirth is probably the first time when your role as a dad will become truly tangible.

As a result, you may have to 'catch up' to your partner by interacting with your baby and internalizing your role in order to form that bond. It's not that you're worse at it... you're just behind.

For some dads, their baby's birth can also trigger a 'protect and provide' instinct, which is good, but when you couple it with the societal influences I've already mentioned, it can interfere with bonding by motivating you to be a detached 'breadwinner' at the expense of meaningful time with your kid.[8]

One of the reasons this can affect a dad's bond with his baby is that some of those hormonal changes I described earlier are influenced by how much contact you have with your child and your partner.[9]

If you're out working all day and not being intentional about having solo care-giving time with your newborn when you get home in the evening, it's actually going to impact your biology. One study by an endocrinologist at Memorial University in Newfoundland says that the hormonal changes that dads experience during their baby's initial stages of life end once they have less physical contact.[10]

By not being hands-on with your baby from the start, you'd be missing out on a particularly valuable time in their lives.

Bonding With Infants: Practical Tips for Dads

Even if you still have some self-doubt about your ability to bond with your newborn or are particularly hampered by some of the societal influences we've discussed, there are tricks to making bonding with your newborn easier.

Tip 1: Talk to Your Baby… Even Before She's Born

By about 24 weeks, babies can hear sounds from outside the womb and will turn their heads in response.[11] That gives you months before your baby is even born for her to get to know you.

The voice most familiar to unborn babies is naturally that of their mom, but deep, low sounds come through more easily than high-pitched ones. After your baby is born, she'll be able to recognize your voice and respond to it from all the times she heard it in utero.

Tip 2: Keep Up the Communication

After your baby's born, recite nursery rhymes, read her bedtime stories, sing… she doesn't care if you're a little tone-deaf. Oh, and lay off the high-pitched cutesy baby language. Use normal language in gentle tones because this is how your baby starts to develop speech and language skills.

You can use diaper changes as the perfect opportunity to get some interesting conversation going with as much eye contact as possible. Remember it's a two-way conversation, so pause and give her a chance to get in a word edgewise! She'll get when it's her turn to 'make some noises'.

Tip 3: Practice Skin-to-Skin Contact

You may have already heard about the benefits of babies having 'skin-to-skin contact' with mom, especially during the first few weeks of birth. Well, it's just as beneficial when dads do it. Essentially, you'll dress your baby in just a diaper and place him directly on your chest. It'll help to stabilize his blood pressure, body temperature, heart, and respiratory rates. It's also been proven to calm and comfort babies as well as help with bonding—for both moms and dads.[12]

Tip 4: Learn Baby Massage

Baby massage promotes the same 'quiet alert' state that breastfed babies get. That's because breastfeeding works on hand-to-eye coordination (especially if switching sides often) while massage can help improve their coordination and fine motor skills by using simple movements, like crossing their arm over their chest or pulling each individual finger or toe.

It also helps your baby relax and sleep better. Plus, it's a time when they can see, feel and smell you, which is really important to a newborn.

In one study, dads were trained in baby massage techniques. One group of dads was told to massage their one-month-old babies, while the other group was told not to. After two months, the babies that were massaged greeted their dads with much more eye contact, cooing, smiling, and reaching out. They also showed much fewer avoidance behaviors than the babies who were not massaged.[13]

Tip 5: Establish a Routine

By about five or six months old, babies respond well to a schedule because it's comforting to them. Work rituals into your day like breakfast together every morning, a walk after work, or a bedtime story. Try to do these at the same time every day so that you and your baby can come to expect and look forward to them, which will help with bonding.

Don't listen when people insinuate that it's only important for dads to have a close relationship with their kids when they're older and less dependent on their moms.

Parenting isn't a relay race.

Your relationship with your newborn will encourage him to learn, explore, and become more confident and independent later on. The more dads interact with their kids, the better the kids' mental health, language, and academic abilities.

Also, the amount of time you spend playing with your baby has a direct impact on how secure he'll feel growing up, and even on how easily he'll be able to socialize when he starts kindergarten. Forming a strong bond with dad will minimize behavioral problems later in life, maybe even more so than interactions with mom (as we'll discuss in a later chapter).

So, don't let cultural myths, stereotypes, and self-doubt get in the way of building that relationship from day one. It's the bedrock for your relationship with one another for the rest of your lives.

Your son or daughter won't always be waiting for you by the front door when you get home, so don't let their tender years go by. You'll only regret it later if you do.

PART II

COMPETING DEMANDS

4

MARITAL STRESS – DON'T BE NAÏVE

I used to work for a moving company. I still remember one couple in their mid-50s, who I moved because they were under water with their mortgage and needed to downsize after the 2008 housing crisis.

Since they didn't have equity to work with, they bought what they could afford—a ramshackle house built in the 1800s which was quite literally on the wrong side of the tracks.

They were moving out of a very nice brick home three or four times that size, which was located in a good neighborhood. Their new home only had two rooms upstairs and two rooms downstairs, none of which looked like they'd been renovated in the last 150 years.

They'd already sold a lot of their furniture and belongings, but as we unloaded the truck it quickly became clear that there wasn't enough space.

We began stacking box after box around the walls of the bedrooms upstairs. Pretty soon, every wall was stacked floor to ceiling.

Then, we had to start filling in the middle of each room. By the time we were done, three of the four rooms were so full there wasn't enough space to get in the door much less unpack. Part way through the job, I was even worried the floor was going to give way due to the condition of the house, so we rearranged everything to make sure the heaviest items were against the walls.

Early on, I offered that we could unload part of their belongings at a storage facility to make things more manageable, but they didn't want to. When it was all said and done, the lady was in tears, and her husband was overwhelmed.

Sadly, we had no choice but to leave them like that… crying in the kitchen with no clear way forward. They needed to de-clutter their lives, but they were clinging to the past. And now, they didn't even have the space to do the hard work that needed to be done.

Be Honest With Yourself

What's the condition of your relationship with your partner right now? Is it more like that spacious brick home or a dilapidated four-room shack?

How much emotional clutter are the two of you hanging on to? Have you been working through things as they come up, or are the floors about to collapse because of all the relationship baggage?

What does any of this have to do with a baby, you might ask? Well, the single best way for you to be a good father is to have a good relationship with your kid's mother.

Parenting is an emotional pressure-cooker that will put even a healthy relationship to the test.

The relationship between you and your partner is like the foundation of a house. Everything else, including your ability to be good parents, rests on that foundation. So it needs to be sound, else the structure will likely collapse given enough time for nature to do its work.

And, lest naiveté get the better of you, understand that there's no force of nature quite like having a newborn baby. First, you'll face a tsunami of medical bills following childbirth, then the frequent eruptions of ear-splitting wails from a colicky infant, not to mention the daily whirlwind of daycare runs and work commutes.

If your relationship is already characterized by unwavering commitment, openness, mutual respect, and selflessness, a new baby is just going to cement that.

This new shared adventure, with all of its challenges, will just demonstrate what's already present in your relationship and take it up a notch... or ten.

For a relationship where the cracks have already started to show, having a baby is sure to blow them wide open. A new baby is quickly going to expose any underlying commitment issues or selfishness either of you might have, and it's likely to result in frequent and intense blow-ups.

For example, an imbalance in the division of labor between you and your partner, which may have been overlooked before, will become a cause for the first resentment. It can turn into silent contempt when you add the stress and fatigue of caring for a newborn into the equation.

If you and your partner have different ideas about how to balance family and your careers, expect these to become major sticking points once you're sharing parental responsibilities.

Don't Be Naïve – Babies Don't Cure Strained Relationships

My wife and I also know of a few couples who had a baby in the hopes of "fixing" their relationship without putting in the real and painful work of getting to the root cause of the dysfunction and letting go of the past. Not only did it not work, but it had the opposite effect.

If your relationship is rocky to begin with and having a baby doesn't magically fix everything—which it won't —it'll be tempting to use all the added work as the perfect diversion while you drift further apart. Mom is likely to pour her emotional energy into your child as an outlet and replacement for you, whereas you might be more inclined to bury yourself in your work.

What's really dangerous is that this diversion allows the issue to fester for years unaddressed. Then, when it finally comes to a head, it's too late to resolve anything, because neither of you can even remember what the original cause of the conflict was.

Nonetheless, all of the hurt and contempt is still there. I mean, at this point, it either ends in a painful divorce or it continues in a sad detached farce of marriage for the sake of children, who are themselves going to grow up wounded but will need less attention, leaving the two of you as co-habiting strangers.

Thankfully, both of these outcomes are avoidable, but we'll get to that in a moment.

Yes, a Storm is Coming

Even if you think your relationship is strong, don't underestimate the challenges you're going to face; there will be a lot of them!

Once your new baby arrives, the first thing you're going to struggle with is finding enough hours in the day.

Alone time with your partner may seem not only impossible but very low on the priority list. Any lofty ideas you may have had about continuing to be the same couple you were before, with the only addition being a pint-sized bundle to share, will quickly be blown out of the water.

It's not uncommon for new dads to feel a tiny twinge of jealousy when all the attention and affection their partners previously showered on them is funneled into the baby, though this is probably symptomatic of a deeper insecurity in their relationship.

But even for dads who don't experience this, most men will only tolerate so many expressionless commands to pack the diaper bag or check the bottle temperature before they snap back. It's easy to get along when the most important issues you have to decide on are which movie to watch and whether to order Chinese or Italian.

But starting a family raises the stakes considerably. Not only do you have more important issues to disagree about, but you'll be doing it in a state of heightened irritability, caused by sleep deprivation and the increased stress and frustration of caring for a newborn.

Worse still, either you or your partner could suffer from postpartum depression following your baby's arrival. And yes, it hits one in ten new dads, too.[1] Undiagnosed and untreated, this condition can affect everything from your ability to bond with your baby to your relationship with your partner.

Shoring up Your Foundation: Practical Tips

The good news is that your relationship doesn't need to buckle under the pressure, provided the commitment is there from both sides.

You and your partner must be willing to work together in unique new ways to balance parenting with a healthy relationship. The other good news is that the amount of physical and emotional energy your kids need from you decreases the older they get. But it's up to you whether you and your partner have a relationship to fall back on at that time.

Instead of naively thinking that having a baby is going to fix your relational mess or blindly assuming you've got no mess to fix, you'd rather want to approach parenthood expecting it to be a massive test of your relationship and start strategizing on how to address obstacles as early as possible. Better that than going into this new chapter of life overconfident and unprepared only to suffer a rude awakening.

If you become aware of the cracks in your relationship before the baby comes, it's not a deal-breaker, it's a blessing in disguise. Now you have the opportunity to address them and strengthen your foundation before the storm hits.

If you find yourself looking to shore up your family's foundation, there are a number of ways you can do that, both before and after the baby arrives. But do it quickly, and do it properly.

Tip 1: Be Intentional About Communicating

Your best tool will be open, honest communication in the spirit of understanding.

No matter how close you think you and your partner are before your baby comes along, neither of you is a mind reader. If you and your partner absolutely never have any disagreements… that isn't a mark of relational health. It means your relationship likely has cancer because one of you is avoiding conflict and bottling everything up.

Even if you're not feeling the strain, it doesn't mean your partner isn't. Remember, you're not the only one whose life is getting turned upside down, and without you realizing it your partner might be silently struggling to cope. So give her a chance to open up about her frustrations and fears.

Every couple should be intentional about having conversations to identify those unstated areas of apprehension or disagreement before they become areas of open conflict, especially when a baby is on the way.

Tip 2: Bring in a Third Party if You Have to

Counseling can offer you a safe environment and an outside perspective, from someone who has training and experience in helping others work through difficult issues.

I get that it can be pricey to call in the professionals and your health insurance is unlikely to cover it, but it doesn't need to be a marriage counselor. You could approach a local church in your area and find out if they offer free counseling, even to non-members, as part of their service to the community. During the early stages of our relationship, my wife and I availed ourselves of help from lay counselors on numerous occasions and it saved our marriage.

Taking a more proactive approach will prevent negative emotions from bottling up and festering into anger and resentment.

It'll also alert you to where you've been selfish, neglectful of your partner's needs, had unreasonable expectations of her, or where the split in responsibilities between you is uneven. So many petty squabbles can be avoided just by both partners being clear about what each expects of the other. Putting your expectations of your partner into words also helps you realize when they're unreasonable and gives you a chance to adjust them. And, it does the same for her, because women can be just as unreasonable as men.

Tip 3: Don't Underestimate the Little Things

Small acts of love and kindness, even on a busy day, can make an immense difference to the atmosphere in your relationship.

Three little words, "I love you," cost nothing, and yet, when you say it to one another intentionally, sincerely, and often, it squashes many unspoken insecurities and anxieties.

Two little words, "Thank you," when your partner does anything for you will make her feel acknowledged and appreciated.

Holding hands, hugging, kissing, and laughing together are important ways to maintain the connection and intimacy in your relationship, so keep doing them. If you've stopped, start again.

Ask (with interest) how your partner's day went. Each of these small gestures is like placing another brick that strengthens your foundation or laying another sandbag to stave off the flood.

Tip 4: Keep 'Dating' Your Partner

You may be lucky enough to have parents willing to babysit one or two evenings per month so that you can go out for dinner on your own. But even if you don't have that option, there are activities you can do as a family that'll keep your kids occupied and give the two of you a chance to connect.

With our firstborn, my wife and I loved going on a walk with the stroller because it gave us the chance to have an uninterrupted conversation and just generally enjoy each other's company. Now, when time permits, we do things like run errands together so we can catch up with each other while the kids are distracted by the radio in the car.

Let's Talk about Commitment

You'd be surprised how quickly the things I just mentioned can improve a strained relationship, but I do have a further word of caution.

It doesn't matter how strong your foundation is if you're building your house on sand. The strongest of foundations can't tolerate the ground moving beneath it, so you need to build on bedrock. When it comes to relationships, that bedrock is called commitment.

At the root of many a troubled relationship is one party feeling that the other is 'keeping their options open'.

Those doubts will destroy trust and sink your relationship.

And let's face it, commitment is an act, and no amount of verbal reassurance is going to cut it. Sometimes, not formally committing is meant to preserve each party's independence, but all it really does is sabotage your relationship.

As long as you're hedging your bets, there's going to be the temptation to cut and run when the going gets tough (and it will).

What's more, even if your partner is ready to commit to you, she might feel she needs to follow suit and hedge her bets to protect herself. Shifting sand. So much for a firm foundation!

I get it. Many people avoid marriage like the plague because the only marriages they've seen or experienced were their parents' (or their own) toxic ones. But we've covered this; you can build a firm foundation if you're committed to putting in the work. That kind of trust and stability becomes even more relevant when you add kids into the equation... and not just for you and your partner, but for the kids themselves.

Once you decide to start a family with your partner, it may be clear to you that your relationship is long beyond a passing fling, but you can't expect it to be clear to her.

And before objecting that your partner and you both agree that it's best not to get married, understand something. That just means it's likely that neither of you are as committed as you should be when starting a family.

Nothing says it better than a marriage contract that you're in it for the long haul. To date, it is the single most significant step a man can take to show that he remains committed and involved as a father, while maintaining a strong family bond.

5

NO SEX – WHO SAID?

W e're still on the topic of you and your partner's relationship, but this section has a slightly different thrust to it. We can't talk about intimacy without addressing what's going to happen to your sex life during and after pregnancy.

And, this isn't an easy topic to discuss with so many misconceptions, unfounded fears, and pub psychologists chiming in on the issue with all of their innuendo and double entendres. Nonetheless, we're going to plumb the depths of this issue by helping you understand the limitations you might face as a couple and how to find your rhythm again once the baby is born.

Puns aside, societal stereotypes would have everyone believe that the extent of a man's thought processes on this subject is no more complex than the hormonal fixations of a teenage boy.

Even some of the other prominent books within this genre play into this idea, joking that readers might want to consider upgrading their internet speed to get their porn fix while their partners are pregnant. One even goes so far as to imply that the urge to have an affair during the third trimester shouldn't be unexpected.

I have no doubt there are many men whose behavior would prove those authors correct. But I'm not one of them, and I have enough regard for you, as a man, to assume that you're not either.

For those who are, I'd suggest they go read the previous chapter again.

Now, I don't doubt that almost any man will find the prospect of going without sex for an extended period of time challenging, but the fact is that doing so is rarely necessary. Yes, there will be limitations to what you do under the covers, but with a little creativity, under-standing, and dedication to finding out what works, most couples won't need to experience more than a few weeks of abstinence after the baby is born.

With your first pregnancy, neither you nor your partner know what to expect, and there are a lot of causes for the anxiety about sex during pregnancy that you might experience—first and foremost among them often being concerns for the safety of your partner and child. The reality is, however, that sex during pregnancy is not only safe but helpful for both your baby and your lover, as long as she has a normal, healthy pregnancy without complications.

No, You Won't Hurt the Baby

Between the amniotic fluid and the wall of the uterus muscle in between, your baby is completely safe. He's also not going to get poked in the head or even know what you're up to in the moment.

You should still pay attention to keeping weight and pressure off your partner's belly, but that's mostly during the third trimester and more for her comfort than your baby's safety.

Sex during pregnancy doesn't cause miscarriages either. So long as strenuous activity is no more intense than what your partner is already used to, it won't cause premature labor.

I mean, if a pregnant Serena Williams could win the 2017 Australian Open, I think your partner will be able to handle a roll in the hay.[1]

Don't freak out if your partner notices some blood-spotting after you make love; that's normal too. It's just because the cervix is soft and sensitive and bleeds easily. Now, if the bleeding is excessive and doesn't let up, or if your partner experiences pain during or after sex, none of that should be ignored. She should talk to her midwife or doctor about it.

But, sex during pregnancy isn't just safe... it's beneficial.

Orgasms during pregnancy increase cardiovascular blood flow in your partner's body, which all passes down to your baby. It also helps strengthen her pelvic floor muscles, which could mean an easier and faster recovery after childbirth, as well as her not feeling like she needs to pee as often as the pregnancy progresses.

If your partner is at risk of pre-eclampsia, the proteins in your sperm could lower her chances of developing the condition. Sex during pregnancy also helps prepare your partner's body to go into labor, by exercising her uterine muscles and stretching things out to make the actual birthing process easier. As your partner gets closer to her due date, you can even add 'vigorous cuddling' to your list of ways to encourage labor.

Exploring New Frontiers

A lot of people don't realize that sex during pregnancy can often be even more enjoyable than normal.

For one, since there's neither pressure to conceive nor the 'risk' of conceiving, you can both just enjoy it. The fact that there's no need for you to wear protection certainly has its benefits, but your partner may also have a more pleasurable experience, since her increased blood flow will make her more sensitive than usual in all the right places.

On top of that, her actual orgasm releases the hormone oxytocin. Not only does oxytocin help relieve some of that expectant parent stress, but it's the same hormone that ignites the feeling of lust, so don't be surprised if she wants you more than usual or is especially open to trying new things.

You may also find yourself among the majority of men who find their partner's pregnant body even more attractive than usual.

Not only does she have that pregnancy glow, but her skin looks amazing, and her belly won't be the only feature with more curves during pregnancy. During the third trimester, being on the bottom will give you ample opportunity to appreciate the fruits of pregnancy from a new perspective.

Mileage May Vary

While the odds are good that you'll both want to maintain your sex life throughout pregnancy, if not explore new frontiers, every couple does have a different experience.

On the off chance that you end up being one of those couples, I want you to take a minute and imagine what's going on in your partner's world. Pregnancy is doing a number on her. Her body is going through some pretty significant changes, not least of which are crazy hormones.

While those hormones might be the source of a lot of exciting new 'developments' and sensations for both of you to enjoy, they could also make intimate touch *too* sensitive. It's impossible to predict how they'll affect your partner, so just keep asking her what feels good, and make sure she knows it's okay to be honest. This is the time to get creative to find what works.

Those hormones may also mean that random things make her nauseous.

Even when the morning sickness (it can actually be all day) starts to die down, she might feel like her body is being stretched in different directions. If she looks in the mirror and thinks she's the biggest and most unattractive she's ever been in her life, she'll probably fear never seeing her pre-pregnancy body again. Oh, and she's tired. Exceedingly tired. All the time.

So, as you're enjoying the bounty of novel experiences that her new body offers, let her know how hot you think she is–don't let your thoughts just sit there uselessly in your head. Also, try treating her to a beauty session at a local salon or spa; she's bound to emerge feeling more desirable than she felt going in.

If fatigue is the issue, try to initiate sex on weekend afternoons or early mornings, when she isn't exhausted after a long day on swollen feet. Start monitoring the times of day when her morning sickness seems to subside and work with her body clock.[2]

Also, remember that your partner's body is constantly changing, so what worked and was pleasurable during one month can change drastically by the next.

So what if you're the one who isn't interested in sex?!

This can take some men by surprise, but I don't want you to freak out. As I mentioned earlier, you're going to experience a drop in your testosterone levels during the pregnancy, and afterward, while caring for your newborn.

I'm sure you already know that this change is going to reduce your sex drive, but it just might hit you more severely than the next guy.

Besides that, as a new dad, you've got a lot on your mind. You're about to go into a whole new phase of life with A LOT more responsibility, and you're worried about not messing it up. If you weren't, you wouldn't be reading this book.

And yes, you became a dad from the moment you found out your partner was pregnant, so despite all the research that says sex during pregnancy won't hurt your baby, the protective instinct in you might be insisting otherwise.

In reality, of all men who don't find their pregnant partners attractive, most are dealing with major fears about the future,[3] and stress like that can wreak havoc on your sex drive. Addressing those fears and concerns is what this whole book is about. If you find yourself in this situation, just keep reading, because there's a really good chance that the issues you're wrestling with are going to be addressed, if they haven't been already.

All this likely has nothing to do with your level of attraction for your partner, so don't start questioning your character just yet.

Of course, your partner doesn't know what's happening to you, and it may set her trampolining dangerously to a few conclusions of her own unless you open up. As awkward as it may be, don't be afraid to bring in outside help if you need to kick-start that conversation and get in the habit of speaking freely to her. Being able to share your fears and concerns more broadly will draw you closer than anything else, and as you work through those issues together, you'll likely solve any issues you're facing in the bedroom.

You May Both Need That Vacation

Regardless of how passionate your sex life is during pregnancy, you and your partner will be forced to pump the brakes for at least a few weeks once the baby is born.

For one thing, you'll probably find that the little bundle you brought home from the hospital has become the center of the universe. Suddenly, you're both in nurturing mode, with all the accompanying hormones, and the last thing on either of your minds is sex.

You're both exhausted and, while you might still fantasize, it's no longer about how your partner looks in her sexiest lingerie but a seemingly distant time when you could sleep undisturbed for more than 30 minutes.

In your case, the more you interact with your baby, the lower your testosterone levels will get, and consequently, your sex drive will drop. While this might not seem like a good thing to you, it's actually a blessing in disguise because your partner needs time to heal after giving birth; otherwise, sex could be painful, unpleasant, and even dangerous.

While I'm sure you get that you're partner needs to recover, let me pause and elaborate a bit on just what your partner may need to recover from, and I warn you it's not for the fainthearted.

The perineum is the tissue around the vagina, and just before your partner gives birth, this tissue will thin out to get ready for your baby to push through safely. Sometimes, the perineal tissue tears. This could be because your baby is large, or the delivery was too quick for it to stretch.

Tearing can also happen if the doctors use forceps or suction during the delivery—the chances of which are greatly increased if she opts for an epidural. If your partner's vaginal opening isn't wide enough for your baby to push through, the doctor may even perform an episiotomy, which is a controlled cut to widen it. The episiotomy is meant to prevent tearing, but sometimes a tear occurs anyway.

First-degree tears are the least severe and may not even need stitches. Anything from second degree up will need stitches, which usually dissolve after about six weeks, at which point, in theory, you and your partner can safely start having sex again without risk of infection. But sometimes, even after your partner's stitches have dissolved, they can leave a ridge or flap of scar tissue that causes pain during sex, even 4-5 months after childbirth.

Note, though, that this is not just a normal side effect of tearing and can be easily fixed through quick corrective surgery. If your partner does end up feeling this kind of discomfort after pregnancy, she should see a doctor rather than "soldiering on" because it's often a very minor fix.

In addition to giving your lover's lady parts plenty of "exercise" to stretch things out before the baby comes and avoid tearing, taking mega doses of sodium ascorbate (buffered vitamin C) every day during and after her pregnancy will help her heal faster if she does tear. Since vitamin C is needed for your body to make collagen—a fundamental building block of your body's skin, muscles, and other tissues—this could cut down her healing time by over 50%.

Even when your partner has healed physically, she may still suffer the mental and emotional after-effects of vaginal trauma during birth, and her sex drive could take up to six months to return. It's not common, but it does happen.

The good news is that 80-90% of women resume sex with their partners within six months of childbirth.[4] Even more encouraging is that 94% of couples are satisfied with their sex lives after kids, with a whopping 60% saying sex after having a baby is even better than it was before. What's more, 63% of dads said they found their partner more attractive, and another third of them said their partner was just as attractive as before.[5]

That's all well and good, but what if you happen to be among the 10% of men whose partner isn't comfortable having sex, even after six months? What if you're among the 6% of couples who are not satisfied with their sex lives after having a baby?

Well, by virtue of the fact that you and your partner chose to bring a life into the world together, I assume you have a connection that goes beyond the physical to the intellectual, emotional, and spiritual.

Getting Back in The Saddle

If you find yourself taking a longer than expected break from adult playtime, remember that it's not the sex that you need to keep going, it's the intimacy.

There are so many ways to be intimate. Just keep talking and touching. A foot massage, or even just a hug, will release the bonding chemical, oxytocin. The fact is that if the intimacy in your relationship is solely dependent on whether or not you can have sex, then there are deeper issues in your relationship that you and your partner need to address.

Plus, it's not like you're sworn to six months (or even six weeks) of complete abstinence. Chances are that there are only a few activities that are completely off limits. Think outside the box... there are probably plenty of new forms of stimulation that you haven't tried before, which could add an element of excitement and pleasure to your sex life.

Perhaps now is a good time to get creative and explore some things you've never tried, but which will still give your partner the space she needs to heal, physically and emotionally. And then, once you're ready to get back in the saddle, grab whatever opportunities present themselves, most likely when your baby's napping, to show each other that you want to reconnect sexually.

Remember that, in the beginning, you're probably going to need some extra lubricant since your partner's estrogen levels will have dropped quite a bit after childbirth, reducing her natural lubrication.

Your partner could also get a prescription from her gynecologist for an estrogen cream, though this is less advisable for moms nursing baby boys as the estrogen will get in the breast milk and can negatively impact a boy's development.

Above all, open communication, understanding, compromise, and adaptability here are going to be crucial in ensuring that sex is enjoyable for both of you again.

Try not to form expectations of your own experience based on your friends' accounts of their sex lives during and after pregnancy. If you've been reading attentively, by now you know there are a host of factors at play that combine uniquely for each couple and influence their experience.

But, if you manage to keep the intimacy going, there's no reason why you and your partner can't have a sex life after the birth of your baby that is just as hot and steamy as it was at the start of your relationship. You'd be among two-thirds of couples who experience this, according to the largest ever study conducted on the topic.[6]

Getting creative to find what works for you and your partner while dancing under the sheets will serve you well, even beyond the birth of your baby. A willingness to try new things is key to a long and happy sex life.

6

WORK-LIFE BALANCE – YOU CAN HAVE ANYTHING, BUT YOU CAN'T HAVE EVERYTHING

With a baby on the way, you have a lot of hats to wear: involved dad, attentive partner, high-performing employee, etc. And that's assuming you've put every other part of your life on hold.

Yet, our society is still largely stuck in an era where dads are basically viewed as sperm donors and detached providers, and little effort's been made to change the status quo.

Since you're reading this book, I'm pretty sure that you want to be an involved dad just as much as your partner wants to be an involved mom. A recent Pew Research study found that the percentage of dads who considered parenthood as a huge part of their identity was almost equal to that of moms.[1]

But the rest of our society has other ideas because, even today, dads are still viewed mostly as financial providers and moms as involved parents. In fact, that same study found that 76% of Americans think there's a lot of pressure on dads to provide financially, but less than half think there's pressure on dads to be involved parents.

So, there's a good chance you're fighting this huge disconnect between how you see yourself and how society sees you.

In this context, it's not surprising that our culture has failed to appreciate the psychological and emotional effects of dads not being able to take an active role in their children's lives.

Like most dads, you may find that your work demands are real and unforgiving. So, there's a pretty good chance that you'll end up dealing with guilt and frustration when you think you're either dropping the ball on the parenting front or taking just a little too much time off work to spend with your family.

One study found that one in five dads goes through this internal tug-of-war.[2] The results from that Pew Research study mentioned earlier suggest the numbers may be much higher, with over 60% of dads feeling like they're not spending enough time with their kids (vs.

only 35% of moms) and citing work obligations as the main reason for this.

In fact, dads in dual-earner couples are now reporting more work-life balance conflicts than moms![3]

While there's a lot of talk today about working moms' struggle to meet expectations, the reality is that you and your partner are both going to be confronted by these competing demands.

It's just going to hit you in different ways.

Your partner, like most moms, could end up being responsible for the bulk of childcare and have to make some significant career sacrifices. We hear a lot about that, but the flip side of that narrative isn't really talked about.

While women are more likely to put their careers on hold, the majority of dads feel pressured to keep their focus on work at the expense of being as involved as they'd like with their families.

One study of 1,200 men even found that 63% of working dads envied their stay-at-home counterparts.[4] It's worth noting that careers *can* be put on hold, but you'll *never* get a second chance to hear your son's first words or see him take his first steps.

My point is not in any way to diminish the very real sacrifices that moms make for their kids—after all, this isn't a contest. Rather, I'm putting into words what a lot of men are already thinking or sensing, even if they're not entirely sure where those feelings are coming from.

'Dispensable' Dads – What a Harmful Myth

For all the messaging from various quarters of our society claiming to promote 'involved' dads (as if dads didn't want to be involved), there certainly doesn't seem to be much genuine interest in helping men balance their other commitments and play a more active role in raising their kids day-to-day. There is, however, a lot of patronizing and false praise for dads who change exactly the same number of diapers as their partners, offset with criticism for dads whose work and life circumstances don't permit such a scrupulously equal division of care-giving responsibilities.

The unpopular truth is that a lot of moms' greater involvement in early childcare, like nursing and the actual birth, comes down to basic biology. The rest is the product of a society that treats dads' involvement with their children as 'dispensable' and 'negotiable'.

I mean, just compare parental leave policies for employees with new babies. Dads bonding with their newborn babies is nowhere on the priority list, and the statistics back it up.

Sure, big companies like the Fortune 500 in the US are supposed to house some of the world's most respected thought-leaders, but somehow these captains of industries still haven't gotten around to recognizing the importance of father-child bonding time in the lives of young kids.

A recent report on 353 Fortune 500 companies found that 72% have some form of paid parental leave, which is great, but nearly half of them offer at least twice as much paid leave to moms as they do to dads.[5]

But disparities in parental leave don't stop with the amount of parental leave offered; they extend to whether or not leave is even paid when it is available. In the US, only 45% of dads get any paid parental leave, compared to 55% of moms.

And if those disparities didn't make things hard enough for dads to be engaged from day one, some companies insist that parental leave shouldn't affect employees' work schedules. Hard to imagine even the token amounts of leave offered to dads not affecting their work schedules, so it's no wonder most dads only take about a week off work when their babies are born.

And it's not as if dads in the UK fare much better. Moms in the UK receive up to 52 weeks of maternity leave, with the first six weeks paid at 90% of their salary and the remainder at the minimum statutory maternity pay rate.[6]

Moms can share this leave with their partners, but the uptake on that has been low for several reasons. For one, there's an economic incentive not to share leave because the joint household income is often far less if the benefit is shared than if dads continue working to earn their full salary. There's also the issue of men, understandably, not wanting to be perceived as "robbing" their partners of this precious leave.

Balancing Work and Fatherhood: Practical Tips

Let's pause here for a moment.

Over half of working dads find it challenging to balance work with family.

A lot of this has to do with cultural perceptions that are anything but affirming and encouraging of dads actually being involved parents. You know that already. As a dad who does want to be involved, it's an overwhelming struggle, a Herculean task really.

So, what's the solution? What are the 'involved' dads doing? How do they manage, and what's their secret?

Every situation looks a bit different, but those dads who are the most successful do three things well: they work with their partner like a team instead of two individuals who happen to be living together, they learn to say "no" at work instead of sacrificing their families to their career ambitions, and they're intentional about choosing what they're going to sacrifice instead of letting life choose for them.

But before we get into any of that it's important to remember that "involved" is going to look different for every dad. Our culture seems to have defined the "involved" dad as somebody who painstakingly tracks every diaper he changes to make sure he doesn't fall below his strict 50% quota, no matter what the rest of his or his partner's responsibilities look like.

Frankly, that's just nonsense that pits you against your partner without regard for what works best in your family. It weaponizes this arbitrary metric for how "involved" you are, without considering the fact that going to a job that puts food on your family's table and keeps a roof over your family's head is equally a part of being a parent—whether you're a dad or a mom

Suggesting that working dads are somehow not carrying their weight, when they can't assume an equal share of daily childcare responsibilities, is as ridiculous as criticizing working moms who can't breastfeed.

Don't buy into this garbage. You and your partner need to make a conscious decision about what's even feasible for your family and do what will work best for all of you.

If your partner is a stay-at-home mom and you're the primary breadwinner, it's not reasonable to think you're going to be changing as many diapers and doing as much laundry. By contrast, you might be the one shouldering the majority of baby-related responsibilities if your partner is working and you choose to be a stay-at-home dad. At its heart, the problem with our society's current narratives about involved fatherhood is that they treat the mom and the dad as separate entities in competition with one another rather than treating them as a team.

So, what does it look like to approach parenting as a team in a world that pits moms and dads against one another?

Tip 1: Time is a Joint Resource, so Start Acting Like it

For one, to join the actively involved half, you and your partner will need to work together to form a well-oiled tag team. Perhaps the biggest key to this is to start viewing your time as a mutual resource and distribute it cleverly and with love and consideration to ensure that each of you succeeds.

Strategize and prioritize all responsibilities so that you both have a say in who does what and when. You both need to make sacrifices so that neither of you carries too much of the load alone. This doesn't mean that your responsibilities are always going to be identical, but it does mean that your partner's successes in this effort are yours too, and yours are hers.

The same is true with your failures... they're shared.

Because you're both invested in maximizing your joint time resource, the odds are that you'll both end up saving time by working more efficiently and have a better quality of life as a couple than if you struggled along as individuals. If you're not already doing this, start working together to save time now so that these habits are already part of your lives when the baby gets here. When your baby is born, time will be in significantly shorter supply.

Don't think that this division of responsibilities will simply fall into place based on the tasks you're each interested in or skilled at doing. Sure, it may be wise to assign tasks based on those considerations initially, but this doesn't work unless there's open communication and flexibility.

Remember that even something you initially enjoy and are good at can become a rigid expectation and a source of resentment when you don't get a break from it. Plus, if you each only ever do what you're good at, neither of you gets to grow into a well-rounded parent by mastering new skills. Maintain an openness to switching things up to even out any imbalances before they become a source of conflict.

That reminds me of a friend who had a more flexible work schedule than her fiancé, making her the point-person for picking up their little one from day-care every day.

Over time, she started feeling resentful that she had no space to fit anything else in during the afternoon while her fiancé was religious about working out at the gym every day.

Of course, there's a wrong way to tag-team with your partner, too. We have another friend who's a stay-at-home mom while her husband works a full-time job. This lady expects her husband to become the sole care-giver as soon as he walks through the door each evening so she can have a "break".

Not only are both arrangements doomed in the long run, but they're also guaranteed to breed contempt and endanger your relationship. Your expectations of each other need to be reasonable for this to work.

Speaking of work, while I'm encouraging you to break down any walls that prevent you and your partner from functioning as a team, there are some firm boundaries that you should build around your family time in other areas. You need to do this to protect it from other demands, like those of your employer, for instance.

Tip 2: Learn to Say "No"

If your employer is in the habit of encroaching on your personal life outside of work hours, you must learn to say "no".

Then, make a point of leaving on time every day. Firstly, so that you're not expected at a whim to work extra hours and, secondly, so you don't use work as an excuse to avoid your responsibilities at home.

Once you leave work, keep your phone and email notifications off until the following morning when you're getting ready to go to the office. It sends a clear message that your family time is off-limits. You can also use a common calendar for work and family so that conflicting dates don't interfere with important family events and duties, like birthdays, anniversaries, and family outings or picking up your child from day-care when it's your turn.

However, sometimes, no matter how many boundaries you try to put in place, your job could be so all-consuming that it leaves little to no time for family. Well, that may be your cue to consider a career change.

Remember when I said I had gotten my dream job as an intelligence officer just as I became a new dad?

As attractive as the job had looked to me before, the second I became a dad, my lens changed, and I realized that my career trajectory, which would've involved long-term overseas assignments without my family, might need to change. I didn't want to admit it to myself, but that was a big part of what I had to process when my wife told me the good news.

Even on a day-to-day basis, my job would've kept me away from my home during most of my children's waking hours. Before becoming a dad, I hadn't thought through those details with any real specificity, so I underestimated the costs. Once it was clear that my job would cost me my family, I put together a two-year plan to switch careers.

I changed jobs within the organization, gained work experience in a role that was more useful in the private sector, and then made the switch.

Looking at my family now, I know that was one of the best decisions of my life.

Balancing your work responsibilities with being a hands-on dad is going to take a lot of creativity and planning, even if it doesn't require a complete career change. You'll have to fit bonding time in wherever you can. So, instead of stopping off at the store on your way home from work, pick up the family and turn it into a quick outing to the mall.

Sift out the necessary daily tasks from the unnecessary ones. For instance, bathing babies every single day is unnecessary—it can dry out their sensitive skin anyway. Alternate a full bath with a light wash and massage with baby oil, and have a good routine going for feeds, diaper changes, naps, and bedtime.

If you have more money than time, consider hiring someone to clean the house and help with yard work every so often. These time-saving strategies will allow you to spend more quality time with your kid every single day.

Personally, between working a full-time job, running a business on the side, and doing all my own house renovations, I can vouch for how hard it is to make sure you're giving your kids the time they need. For me, having a predictable bedtime routine where I get to read a book to each of my kids, sing to them, pray with them, and tuck them in is invaluable. It guarantees that they'll get at least 30 minutes of my undivided attention every day, regardless of what's going on.

That kind of stability is vital for kids!

With all that being said, I hate to break it to you, but no matter how efficiently you and your partner work together as a team, how carefully you try to plan and problem-solve; regardless of setting boundaries, there are real limits to managing the competing demands of work and family.

Tip 3: Choose What You Will Sacrifice

You can have practically anything, but sadly you can't have everything.

Part of the messed-up narrative that our society promotes these days is that caring for your kids is a burden, but having a "career" is somehow always fulfilling. For a majority of people, though, their "careers" end up just being jobs that put food on the table.

The reality is that every responsibility has its blessings that we take for granted and its drawbacks that make the grass look greener on the other side of the fence.

Yes, spending all day with toddlers can be exhausting, but it's normally no more exhausting than working for a boss that you hate, giving up the best years of your life chained to a desk in a cubicle farm, or putting in long hours on a construction site in 100-degree heat. And, yes, having a career that you love can be fulfilling, but probably not as much as being able to build a relationship with your kids, make memories with them, and enjoy their childhood, which you'll never get back.

It's important that moms and dads both recognize this fact. You'll both have to make some sacrifices along the way, and as a couple, you'll need to choose what you can afford to let go of from the life you had before having a family. It's time to trim the fat.

I can't emphasize this part enough: if you don't choose what you're willing to sacrifice, life is going to choose for you, and that's when the most valuable things are lost, the kinds of things you can never get back.... like your family and being a part of your kids' lives as they grow up.

I'm not saying you can't have a successful career and a healthy family. You only have to set reasonable expectations. Understand at the outset that you and your partner can't both be C-suite executives and still expect to have confident, well-adjusted kids. Something's got to give, and a lot of being a good parent (or spouse) is about self-sacrifice.

My wife has a family member with four daughters and a job that had him working more than 60 hours a week his entire career. He was determined to balance his passion for his career and his goal of becoming an executive, alongside his commitment to keeping his family solid. It was a tall order, and already the divorce rate for people in his particular field was astronomically high.

But even with those odds, he ultimately succeeded on both counts becoming one of the most senior people in his organization and still managing a close relationship with his four, now-adult, daughters and his wife.

How? Well, he put his success down to three critical factors:

- His wife didn't have any serious career ambitions and was happy to be a stay-at-home mom while their kids were younger.
- They were financially able to hire help around the house to lighten the load for his wife while he worked extra-long hours.
- And, he made a conscious decision to sacrifice pretty much every type of leisure activity that didn't involve his family. For instance, he didn't read for pleasure and didn't watch movies,

unless it was with his family. He didn't meet up
with friends outside of work, nor did he watch
or play sports, and he forfeited any hobbies.

Even with all that, though, I've heard him more than
once express regret that he didn't have more time
playing with his children when they were little girls.

I want you to walk away from this section knowing
that balancing work and family life isn't a pipe dream;
it can be done! But I'm not going to pretend that the
advice and tips I'm sharing here will always turn out
like a fairytale.

Some of this is going to come down to you and your
partner making good choices about what to sacrifice
because it's likely that you *will* have to sacrifice. And
much of it will come down to you putting in the work
as well as a willingness to speak openly, listen to each
other, and make sacrifices that work for your family
rather than taking your cues from our culture.

PART III

UNHAPPINESS

7

IDENTITY LOSS – WHY NEW DADS SHOULD IGNORE 76% OF AMERICANS

A while ago, my wife and I were visiting a couple we're friends with. We were explaining how we're in a very busy stage of life right now, and I figure the lady was trying to encourage my wife when she commented, "A mother's job is never done. Now a man's ends at 6 PM, but a mother's job is never done!"

For a second, I thought she was kidding, but her expression said she was dead serious.

Even though her comment didn't sit right with me, I left it alone and the conversation moved on. I knew she meant well, and to be fair, who hasn't heard or said something similar before?

It turns out, though, that the comment hadn't just 'triggered my sensitive male ego', because, on the way home, my wife brought it up all on her own.

Apparently, it had bothered her, too.

It was another manifestation of the cynical stereotypes about dads that seem to sneak in everywhere these days. These stereotypes undermine the necessity of parents working together as a team and pit parents against each other by implying that dads are less necessary than moms for raising happy, healthy kids. They imply both that dads are not interested in being involved in their kids' lives and that their involvement is dispensable.

This couldn't be further from the truth for almost every dad whom I personally know.

As we unpacked why this comment struck us both the way that it did, we realized how profoundly even our friend's unintentional choice of words perpetuated these ideas. She said, "A mother's job is never done, but a man's ends at 6 PM." Not a "father"... just a "man". It's almost as if this "man" doesn't have kids... it's assumed that being a dad isn't part of his identity. It says that being a parent is reserved for the woman in the household because she's the only one equipped for parenting—the only one who really wants to be involved with her kids or who could possibly do a good job.

My wife admitted that this sentiment pretty commonly surfaces in conversations, even among her girlfriends who clearly do value fatherhood.

She told me about how some of her friends often make backhanded compliments about their husbands like, "He actually managed to get the kids to bed, even with their pajamas on, despite only calling me three times during our girls' night out!"

I imagine these comments are usually met with good-natured laughter and then dismissed as harmless. But that's why they're so destructive because they're so commonplace that they infect our language, our jokes, our TV shows without anyone batting an eyelid. And all the while, they're devaluing fatherhood because dads are expected, almost by definition, to be second-rate parents.

"Father Wanted... Men Need Not Apply"

People wonder why becoming a dad might send some men into a full-blown identity crisis.

Before becoming dads, many men pour their time and effort into work and other pursuits where their capability isn't underestimated, and their efforts are valued.

They even face major life changes with added responsibilities, like accepting big promotions at work, commanding combat units, or flying passenger jets, for example.

So, why don't those changes plunge most men into an identity crisis?

It's partly to do with the scale of the change but also with how much our society undervalues a man's efforts when it comes to fatherhood versus more "suitable" aspects of a man's identity, like his career.

For one thing, there's a certain structure to those other changes and responsibilities that make them more predictable and contained. By contrast, fatherhood leaves almost no part of your previous identity untouched. Also, unlike fatherhood, the efforts you put into navigating those changes come with well-understood incentives, like increased salary, rank, and prestige.

Then, you become a dad and you're expected to redirect all that effort towards a role for which society has already weighed men in the balance and found us wanting. Before we've even begun, we're prejudged as "failures" in a role for which we're predestined but which society has decided only mothers are qualified to fulfill.

The societal stereotype is so embedded that, despite all the evidence showing that dads today are more involved and engaged with their kids than the generation before them, only 24% of adults from a Pew Research study thought that today's dads are doing a better job than their fathers did.[1]

Looking at it from a different angle, the general adult population in the US is 11 times more likely than dads themselves to say today's fathers are doing a <u>worse</u> job than the prior generation.

That's an astounding discrepancy! Apparently, us dads think we're doing a pretty good job on average (which is largely backed up by the statistics on father involvement), but pretty much everybody else thinks we're failing miserably.

Even our successes at fatherhood are deemed too unbelievable to be validated with recognition because they don't tie in with the stereotypes of Homer Simpson and Everybody Loves Raymond.

As with almost any other major change in life circumstances—like going to college, getting a job, getting married, etc—becoming a dad means adopting a whole new set of skills, personality traits, habits, and values compared to what you've built your identity around up to this point. Additionally, some of the skills you've built up over the years, maybe even the ones you pride yourself on (like always being the last one to leave the office), will have to be shelved because trying to apply them as a dad could have disastrous consequences.

Understanding Identity Crisis in Fatherhood

With any major life change, this identity "loss" results in a lack of perceived continuity with your past self, which is the basis of the identity crisis that some new dads experience.

Even under normal circumstances, the more you have to let go of from your old life and who you thought you were, the greater your risk of an identity meltdown. This effect is only amplified in a context like I've just described where the positive incentives that should come with that new part of your identity—like being recognized for your importance and efforts as a dad—are displaced by society with a general sense of criticism, inadequacy, and disregard.

People tend to live up to the expectations that others have for them.

Whether you're a student, an athlete, an employee, or a dad, if you're constantly criticized as a failure, that'll often shake your confidence, making it hard to succeed in that particular aspect of your life or to embrace it as part of your identity.

It would help if you had community support.

Having strong friendships with other dads, who have a healthy perspective about fatherhood, can do a lot to combat the toxic messaging from the rest of our society.

Unfortunately, we also live in a society that's moving steadily towards more superficial connections with social media 'friends' and fewer real friends who'll be there when the going gets tough. Let's face it, when the rubber hits the road, a couple of hundred virtual hugs and care emojis are just not going to cut it.

In a 1985 study, people could name at least three close friends, yet a similar study 25 years later found that almost half of people only report having one good friend. [2] I don't want to think about where that leaves us even 10 or 15 years from now.

Seeing through our society's subtle, toxic messaging about dads and the real devastation caused by fatherless households isn't easy. But, once you do, you'll realize that being a dad will probably be the most important role of your life. You'll realize that these stereotypes and the implied expendability of fathers are all a lie, disproved by a mountain of documented evidence to the contrary.[3]

How does the lie manage to persist then?

Well, it's often politically motivated. I mean, historically and across cultures, dads were always considered essential to the household. Unfortunately, the empowerment of women seems to have taken a wrong turn over the years towards portraying men (and therefore dads) in a negative light.

Since masculinity became associated with the oppression of women, the media, politicians, and Hollywood considered themselves 'forward-thinking' by promoting the idea that women don't need a man to raise children and dads are generally lazy and incompetent. Let's hope that society moves away from this misguided belief that to celebrate women and motherhood requires us to diminish the role of dads within the family structure.

Until then, ignore them.

Overcoming Identity Loss in New Dads: Practical Tips

Clearly, as a new dad today, you have a lot to contend with: negative societal stereotypes, all-consuming changes to your life requiring large-scale sacrifice, and a marked lack of community support.

All this paints a pretty bleak picture of the transition to fatherhood. So, what should you do?

Rip it up and paint a new one.

Remember what I said about effort and attitude? Ignore the political and societal trash talk about fatherhood. The statistics point to this being the most valuable role of your life because there's a list as long as my arm of the negative outcomes for kids with an absent father.[4]

As a dad, you're going to interact with your child in a way that is unique, different from the way moms interact with their kids, and equally indispensable.

When you play with your kids, you're stimulating them mentally and physically. You're teaching them self-control and how to regulate their emotions. You're preparing them to know how to take instruction from teachers and lecturers and respond to authority figures for the rest of their lives.

Plus, your cues are going to come from your kids themselves, especially when they're little.

To walk into a room and have it erupt in excited squeals from pint-sized fans is to know you're indispensable to your kids. That explains why dads are equally as likely as moms to consider parenting an extremely important part of their identity.[5]

While not every man experiences the sense of identity loss that I've been talking about when he becomes a dad, it's more common than you might think—even among men who are excited about this new stage of life.

And, for those new dads who do feel this way, it's often difficult to pinpoint the reason why. That's why I've spent so much time focusing on the narratives and cultural influences that have declared war on new dads, often without them even knowing it.

Constant bombardment with this nonsense is at the root of many dads' insecurity and feelings of identity loss.

If you don't recognize these lies, you might end up swallowing them without realizing it... just like my wife's friends do. And, whether you realize it or not, they can wreak havoc on your confidence and ability to be the awesome father that you're made to be.

But, as I've said, cultural messaging isn't the only influence at play here.

Becoming a dad is a big deal, and it's going to require a very real adjustment in how you view yourself. Stereotypes that belittle dads are not the source of the disruption, they just make navigating it that much harder. Recognizing and refuting those stereotypes may be all that some men need in order to embrace their new role with confidence. Others are still going to have some internal work to do to come to terms with the life changes they're going to experience as they successfully navigate their way into fatherhood.

Regardless, a lot of first-time dads have the idea that becoming a dad means completely giving up your prior identity and replacing it. Thankfully, that's not true.

I want to spend the rest of this chapter offering you some practical advice on how to work through any lingering feelings of identity loss that you might be experiencing.

Tip 1: Pinpoint the Source of Your Fear and Loss

Perhaps the best advice I can give is to pinpoint the source of what you're feeling. Instead of wallowing in a general sense of fear and identity loss, spend some time figuring out which of the potential changes that fatherhood brings to your life are scaring you the most. Also, know that almost all of these hit harder in the case of an unplanned pregnancy.

Your identity is a complex thing, so you're going to have to unpack it into its different parts. Here are a couple of areas that you should spend time thinking about:

- *Relational identity*: This is based on your relationships with other people, not just your partner but your friends and family too. We covered the impact of having a baby on your relationship with your partner and how to navigate it. But the fact is that you're going to have less time to give to your other relationships, too, and it's going to be difficult relating to friends who don't have kids. Your really good friends are going to stick around anyway. But you'll probably find that you spend more time with other couples who have kids.

- *Professional Identity*: When you introduce yourself to people, odds are you'll lead with what you do for a living. We spend most of our daylight hours at work, so a lot of our sense of purpose and identity can easily revolve around our jobs. The impact of a career change or becoming a stay-at-home parent on your identity can't be underestimated.

- *Financial Identity*: Having kids can be expensive, whether you move from a dual income to a single income household or not. Even if you and your partner both return to work after parental leave, there'll be an increase in bills and childcare costs. So, while you can save a ton of money by using the tips I give you elsewhere in this book, you're not going to maintain the lifestyle you had before the arrival of your baby.

- *Physical Identity*: A new baby is, without a doubt, going to cut into your gym time. You might be worried about getting a 'dad bod'. But with a little creativity, planning, and teamwork with your partner, it's possible to keep fit and eat healthily, even with a baby in the house.
- *Outlook*: Parenting is a long-term commitment, so it can feel like nothing will ever be the same again. Most of this is going to come down to whether you see fatherhood as an interruption to your life or the most important phase of it. Fear of the unknown is also at play here. Since you've never done this before, you don't know what to expect, and it's easy to mistakenly project your child's needs as an infant out over the next 18 years.

Once you've unpacked the different parts of your identity, you can deal with the fear and disruptions to each part more effectively.

Over the years, I've come to appreciate that men need to talk about their emotions just as much as women do, without fear of being considered weak. Sensitivity is part of being human.

Tip 2: Share Your Fears with Your Partner

Open up to your partner about how you're feeling because it's going to make it easier for you to identify and deal with your fears. Don't suffer in silence, worried that your partner will think you're weak or doubt your excitement about being a dad.

You'll probably find that your partner has the same anxieties. You can be 100% committed to, and even excited about, becoming a dad while still feeling uncertain; the two are not mutually exclusive.

As an added benefit, being open and honest with each other will bring you closer under circumstances that can easily cause you to grow apart. It's easier to integrate your new identity when you're working through these changes with somebody who already understands your importance and values your role.

Tip 3: Connect with Other First-Time Dads

Something else I'd recommend is to reach out to other new dads and create a network for yourself.

You'll find that they're probably in the same boat as you: feeling uncertain and unprepared to suddenly take on the shared responsibilities of caring for a newborn while at least some of what they valued about themselves seems to be threatened.

You also need mentoring and support from other, more experienced dads. Use the benefit of their hindsight about what worked and what didn't to help you navigate your new role as a dad, partner, and provider. If companies understand the value of support and mentoring during a 'workplace promotion', how much more should communities support new dads to fulfill what may be their single most important role in life?

Tip 4: Write Down What You're Afraid of Losing

Another exercise I'd recommend for any man who's feeling an intense sense of identity loss is to start writing down the things you fear losing.

There are some things you'd probably need to let go of anyway, even if you weren't becoming a dad, so do this with someone you trust, like your partner, who knows you best. Once you've crossed off those things that need to go, you can start working out how to incorporate what's left into your new life as a father, even if on a smaller scale.

This is another area where it can be really helpful to have a network of more experienced dads to call on for mentoring and support, especially ones who seem to have struck a good family-work-life balance. They'll help you set more realistic expectations and tell you about the positive experiences you have to look forward to so that you can start forming a positive image of your future self as a dad.

Having a baby doesn't change who you are; it highlights your good qualities and intensifies them.

It also brings out your worst qualities, and when it does, it presents you with the opportunity to work on them. No doubt becoming a father involves a major identity shift, but it doesn't mean you need to wrap yourself up so completely in the new role that you lose your sense of self.

Kids grow up and leave home eventually, and when that happens, make sure you have a sense of purpose and a fulfilling relationship with your partner to fall back on.

Most importantly, don't forget to use the valuable parenthood lessons you've learned to guide a new generation of young men transitioning to fatherhood.

8

CHAOS – "HE POOPED ON THE FLOOR!"

J ust imagine.

You and your partner are at a family member's wedding, seated across from your Aunt Susan. "Best not to wait too long," she insists, while grilling you both about your plans to start a family.

You open your mouth to offer some vague defense, but you're too distracted by your cousin Greg's futile attempts to console his bawling two-year-old daughter, whose cupcake just hit the ground face down. At that exact same moment, hidden from his view, his five-year-old son is bracing himself to yank the cloth from a fully-loaded drink table.

"Sorry to disappoint, Aunt Susan, but it's going to be a really, REALLY long wait."

There's nothing that can put you off having kids more than seeing other parents have public kid drama. And that doesn't touch some of the incidents you'll experience in your own home.

One morning a couple of years ago, before my second son was potty trained, my oldest son shook me awake in bed declaring, "He pooped on the floor!"

Sure enough, I made my way upstairs to my kids' bedroom, and there it was on our hardwood floor, right next to the crib. My son was standing in bed with his diaper off, proudly grinning from ear to ear. That's one of those moments in life that makes you stop and contemplate, "What have I done?"

Stop Believing Urban Legends

But not so fast.

When you're living the carefree life of a DINK ("double income, no kids"), it can be very tempting to pass on all the inconveniences of parenthood. The problem is, you may end up foregoing what many people (myself included) would tell you is the most important, fulfilling, and meaningful experience of their lives... even with the occasional steamer that you have to clean up.

Before you have kids, the only thing on which you have to base your expectations of what it's like to be a dad are the toddler meltdowns you've seen in grocery stores and your coworkers' comically tragic parenting stories about legendary blow-outs and the like. But these are not anywhere close to the whole picture, so they give you a terribly skewed view of fatherhood.

Normally, the best parts of being a dad are either not talked about at all or they're nearly impossible to communicate in a way that's relatable for someone without kids.

How can I possibly explain to a person without children how rewarding it is to influence the life of another human being so profoundly—that every major relationship and experience in your kids' lives will be colored by their interactions with you from the moment they're born? How can I communicate that being a dad makes you grow as a person to become more gracious, more patient, and more perseverant... how it brings the most important aspects of life into focus in an instant?

I can't.

Some things cannot be understood fully until they're experienced. And, frankly, it wouldn't be welcome for me to talk about these things in most contexts, anyway, especially if the man I was talking to wasn't a dad.

Yes, these things are a tremendous responsibility, which some men might also find stifling, but we'll talk more about that in the next chapter. For now, I just want to drive home the point that nothing worth having in life comes without a lot of work and inconvenience.

Do you really think you're going to get a six-pack if you can't push through the initial pain of working out? Would you get a shot at that promotion if you couldn't get over your ear-splitting alarm clock and the detestable rush-hour traffic to get to work on time? Would you even be with your partner right now if you balked at the risk of rejection?

Raising kids is no different. To let the short-term inconveniences of parenthood rob you of the sense of purpose, accomplishment and life-long satisfaction that parenting can bring, is a recipe for an unfulfilled life.

With that in mind, let's dispel a few of the usual, off-putting myths about parenting that you've either been throwing around yourself or had thrown at you.

Myth #1: I'm unique in my dislike for X, Y, or Z.

You might think you have a 'special' intolerance for certain things that you associate with kids, which disqualifies you from being a parent.

Come on!

No matter how much they love their kids, I've never met a parent who's happy about dirty diapers, clutter, deafening wails from a colicky baby, or sleep deprivation. If they were, I'd suspect an imminent breakdown.

This is like a teenager thinking he's just not cut out for college or work because he's put off by the prospect of having to wake up early, dress in uncomfortable clothes, and take instructions from his professor or boss.

When I was a teenager, I remember one of my older brothers saying he never wanted to have kids. "All they do is poop and cry," he'd say.

He was a young bachelor in the military back then. Now, 15 years later, and a proud father of two beautiful daughters, I doubt he remembers ever having dirty diaper anxiety.

Myth #2: This is a life sentence

In reality, the period of time when having kids seems the most chaotic and overwhelming (lack of sleep, noise and whining, a messy house, dirty diapers, etc) is all over in a few short years, while the blessing of having kids lasts for a lifetime.

And even then, exactly how chaotic and overwhelming things are is influenced by the decisions you make as a parent.

One morning, after a particularly exhausting night with my colicky first-born, I remember complaining to my brother (who didn't have kids at the time), expecting just a little brotherly empathy. His response was, "... And you're not nice to be around when you don't get sleep." In that moment, it hit me that I could have gone to bed earlier. Instead, I expected my newborn to fit in with my sleep schedule and ended up more frustrated than I needed to be.

A lot of being a dad is like this. We've also got plenty to learn, not just our kids.

Myth #3: All kids are just brats

Whatever horror stories you've heard or seen in the candy aisle of the grocery store obviously involved entitled, demanding, bratty kids who tyrannize their parents. But you can take comfort here and now in the knowledge that children can be *brat-proofed*.

In fact, the bratty behavior you see is almost certainly a result of the indulgent parenting style of that responsible adult, whom you've pegged as the innocent victim.

A good dad (or mom) puts their child's needs ahead of their own. But here's where parents tend to miss the boat. Wants and needs are two very different things. If you don't distinguish between what your kids want versus what they need, you're going to find yourself indulging their every whim at the expense of everything else, including your wallet and your sanity—a slave at the beck and call of pint-sized tyrants.

The things that kids need change based on the stage of life that they're in. But what all kids need are the intangibles: love, encouragement, and to feel protected. They don't need designer shoes, iPads, or cash incentives to get good grades or score goals.

So, whether you're indulging your kids' whims to see 'the delight on their face' or whether it's just to silence their incessant whining, you're not doing them any favors. Not only is this unnecessary, it leaves you in a financial hole and with nothing but a brood of selfish brats devoid of gratitude, self-control, and empathy to show for it.

Beware the stereotype, though: bratty kids don't always come from parents who throw money at them and ignore them otherwise.

Even with a loving, involved parent who tries to do everything right, it's pretty normal for a kid to still throw the mother of all tantrums from time to time. The point is, it's completely curable. You can train them out of their immaturity, as long as you're willing to stick to your guns, patiently and with love.

It's natural to want to give your kids everything you've never had. But we already live in a society that values people based on their bank balance. Do you really want to perpetuate that message by teaching your kids to measure how much you value them (or worse, how much they're worth!) by how much you spend on them? Giving your kids what they want might just be easier, especially when you don't have the energy to argue with them or listen to them cry or whine. However, you can rest assured, taking the easy way out now will come back to bite both of you later.

Instantly getting what they want means your kids never learn self-control, patience, gratitude or consideration for others. And while you may choose to let them get away with it, you're setting them up for a rude (possibly traumatic) awakening in the world outside of your home where they won't get very far without those qualities.

Parents love their kids, so even when they're annoying, it doesn't change the way parents feel about them. But other people aren't wired to unconditionally love and care about your kids the way you do, so when they step out of line, they're bound to experience rejection. And not only will it blindside them, it won't be their fault.

In the same vein, teaching kids the value of working for what they want is not child abuse. It's a crucial life skill that they'll need to be successful. Theodore Roosevelt said: *"Nothing in the world is worth having or worth doing unless it means effort, pain, difficulty... I have never in my life envied a human being who led an easy life. I have envied a great many people who led difficult lives and led them well."*[1]

Instilling this value in your kids isn't going to be easy; it's going to take being patient with them, taking the time to teach them, and giving them some leeway to learn in due time.

Managing the Chaos: Practical Tips

Now, the myths about having kids are one thing, but there are some very real aggravations that come with parenting young children. The good news is that all of them can be mitigated by using a few clever strategies.

Tip #1: Potty Train Early

We've already talked about potty training, but it bears repeating… dirty diapers don't need to take over your life or your wallet, at least not for long. Babies are born ready to be toilet trained, despite what the diaper companies will have you believe. You don't need to wait until they're able to tell you they're "ready" in grammatically-correct sentences using Oxford Standard English.

As with everything else you teach a small child, so long as you're patient and understanding, potty training your kid early will not be 'traumatic' for them. They know full well when they need to pee and poop, it's you who needs to learn to pick up the little signs they give out.

From my personal experience, start as early as possible. One big benefit of starting early is that babies haven't yet developed that toddler stubbornness, so they're a lot more agreeable to potty training. Plus, it can't be comfortable wearing a soiled diaper, so they have an incentive to cooperate.

After the "power struggle" issues and regression we experienced with our oldest, whom we trained at 25 months, we've trained each of our younger children progressively earlier. Early potty-training helps babies develop self-control, promotes their development of social skills, and builds their confidence and sense of independence.

All those diapers just end up in the dumpster anyway, so buying fewer of them not only saves you a ton of money, but it's also easier on the environment. All things considered, early potty training really is a no-brainer, if you're in a position where you can do it.

Tip #2: Sleep Training is Not Negotiable

Maybe it's not the dirty diapers so much as the expectation of perpetual sleep deprivation that puts you off having kids.

Well, fair enough.

During your baby's first few months, you're going to have many sleepless nights. But guess what. It doesn't last very long. Babies grow, start to interact more, and from as early as four months old many are able to start sleeping through the night.

I say "able" because a big part of whether or not they actually do depends on you, the parents.

A few years ago, I had a co-worker whose son was three or four years old. He and his wife had allowed their son to sleep with them since he was a baby. They finally managed to transition him to his own bed, but he refused to go to sleep unless one of them was lying on the bed with him. If they didn't stay in the room with their son until he fell asleep, he'd scream bloody murder. Every night, putting him to sleep was a process that took more than an hour!

Because my co-worker and his wife were unwilling to be the adults and train their son at an early age, they felt like they were being held hostage, and ended up resenting their kid for it. And that's not me speculating... it was clear in the way he talked about his son while at work.

The truth is, they could've fixed the issue much sooner, been much happier, had much more time on their hands, and had a more loving relationship with their kid if they simply stopped indulging him, established healthy boundaries, and enforced them.

There comes a point, usually when your baby's around four-and-half to five-and-half months old and can sleep for 6-8 hours without needing to feed, when they're ready to start sleep training. And, no, that doesn't mean you lock them in the nursery and let them cry themselves to sleep. All it means is you make sure your baby is dry and fed, then put her down while she's still fully awake so that she can fall asleep on her own.

Not only does this eventually help with putting her down for bedtime or even nap time, but it teaches her to fall back to sleep if she wakes up again.

You decide when she's cried enough to warrant checking in on her and offering a comforting backrub or lullaby. Increase rather than decrease the period you'll let her cry before you intervene by a few minutes each time though. And no, it's not emotionally harmful to your baby; it's probably more traumatic for you than her. But stick it out and be consistent and you'll be glad you did when your sleepless nights become a thing of the past.

Tip #3: Even Toddlers Can (and Should) Clean Up After Themselves

Then there's the issue of ever-present clutter. Having kids means you'll constantly be digging through mess and clutter to find what you need and, when you do, it's bound to be covered in some sort of mysterious filth.

Or does it?

We talked about preparing your child the world outside your home one day, because if you don't, the world is either going to outright reject them for not being properly socialized or will teach them in a way that hits like a bucket of ice cold water.

You have to start teaching junior from an early age about how to exercise respect and consideration for others when they share a space with him. Having chores, however small, strengthens your kid's connection with the family, because he'll feel like a contributing member of the household.

An added perk is that once he knows how much work goes into cleaning and tidying—and that it's his responsibility, too—he'll be less inclined to make a mess in the first place. Start with little duties from the time he's a toddler and work your way up, showing him how while working with him the first few times. Better that than for you to spend the first 10-12 years of his life allowing him to believe he's a permanent guest at the Ritz-Carlton and then, without warning, springing housekeeping duties on him for the first time during his hormonally-charged teenage years.

You want your kids to feel your house is their home, but that doesn't mean you can't have boundaries, unless you want to end up with Lego's and Playdough strewn across your home office desk. It's okay to place expectations on your kids when it comes to cleanliness and order.

Our oldest has always loved to read. Even as a one-year-old, he would take board books off our bookshelf and flip through them himself. After one too many times of stepping over the pile of books in the hallway, we reorganized the shelf so that the books he liked were low enough for him to easily put them back and we encouraged him to do so. By 14 months, he was proudly doing most of the work putting his books back all by himself.

Tip #4: Check Your Own Volume

For me, personally, it isn't the diapers, short periods of sleepless nights, or clutter that's hardest to deal with… it's the noise. No matter how cute you think your kids are, you're going to wish they came with a mute button or at least a volume knob.

Kids are noisy when they're happy, mad, excited, hungry… basically they're noisy when they're awake. And the sounds don't just come from their mouths but from a myriad of beeping, jingling, musical toys they have in their arsenal. Kids will always be noisy to some extent, and they need to have the space to get excited at times; it's a healthy part of their development.

You have to keep in mind that they haven't developed advanced communication skills yet, so they may lack the words to express what they're feeling in the moment. But it's A LOT to contain in a little body, so it has nowhere to go but out… in shrieks!

And, to a point, learning the patience to deal with this is a healthy part of <u>your</u> development; that's something I'm still working on.

At the same time, understand that sometimes when kids scream in the car, shout at the dinner table, and interrupt every conversation you have with another adult, it's just the result of modeling your behavior. I mean, if you're yelling at them to be quiet or to get their attention, they're likely to do what you do, not what you say. There are some tricks that really work to drop the volume though.

Lowering your voice to a whisper is intriguing to little kids; it makes them believe there's something exciting afoot. Every time I whisper to our two-year-old asking her to calm down and stop crying, it's worked, at least for a couple of minutes.

Of course, if nothing exciting follows, the effect wears off, but it usually buys some time, just enough to finish getting her ready for a nap, for example. It also works to get their cogs turning, so when your little ones are overexcited, bring them down by asking them questions.

Clearly, even if you try all the tips I've given you, parenting little children is still going to come with plenty of annoyances and sacrifices. And those aren't going to be unique to you or your kids.

The point is this: don't miss one of the greatest blessings in life because you're scared to get your hands dirty or learn a bit more patience.

Normally, the things you think you'll find so terrible are not nearly as bad as you're imagining. And those things that you will have to deal with can be effectively managed so your life doesn't always feel like a train wreck.

Kids really do grow so quickly, and when the noisy phase is over, replaced by something else, you start to worry that one day they'll be grown up and out, leaving you with a deafeningly silent, spotless house and wishing you could turn the clock back.

9

LOSS OF FREEDOM – NO, IT JUST LOOKS DIFFERENT

I t's not like this was an accident. We'd talked about starting a family at length and made a very conscious decision to do so.

We both wanted kids, and we'd been married for two and a half years, so it seemed like the most natural progression in our lives. No one needed to convince me that having kids was worthwhile.

As I mentioned before, I knew I wanted to have a family even before I met my wife. I was emotionally and psychologically ready for it... or so I thought.

As ridiculous as it sounds now, when my wife announced she was pregnant just five months after we had talked about having kids, it somehow felt like I was losing something.

I could just see our deposit for a house and our dreams of traveling the world taking flight before my eyes… along with my career.

Childish—I know—but it took me three days of mental processing to let my wife know how excited and happy I really was about her being pregnant, and it took me years to figure out why I had such an unexpected response in the first place.

When we discussed trying to start a family, I figured one of us would probably need to quit our jobs or we'd have to pay an arm and a leg for childcare. But, I thought I had more time to figure those things out, so I brushed them aside.

I knew we wouldn't struggle to pay rent or buy groceries, but I hadn't come to grips with what I would have to give up. So, just a few short months later when my wife announced that we were expecting, my imagination took over to fill in the gaps, and it hit me harder than anticipated.

Hearing that we had a baby on the way brought those hazy fears into sharp focus, and they flooded my mind all at once.

Since getting married, we'd hoped to buy my grandparents' old house to keep it in the family, but I was afraid we'd never be able to save enough money to do so after taking on the added responsibility of kids. Despite how much we both hoped to see the world together, I was certain we'd have to put that on hold for at least the next 15 years. And that doesn't touch the unforeseen impacts on my job, with its unique requirements.

While these fears were only uninformed speculation at the time, they felt like dreams that had already slipped out of my grasp.

As people, we feel loss much more intensely than we feel gain, and this is especially true when we don't decide on our own to give up whatever it is that's at stake. In my case, because I hadn't wrestled with these fears beforehand, I hadn't prepared myself to let go of those dreams or to put them on hold, if that were to end up being necessary.

Four kids later, I can see that my fears were rational, but they were overblown. I also realized that the increasingly common notion that children are an unremitting burden is just a symptom of the narcissism epidemic that our society is experiencing.[1] It seems like none of us are immune to the side effects... like the idea that the added responsibilities of becoming a dad will rob us of our freedom to "do what we want".

Experience suggests that reality is quite the opposite.

The Paradox of Responsibility and Freedom

More responsibility does not mean less freedom in this context, or any other.

In fact, you can't have freedom without responsibility because they're two sides of the same coin. More of one almost always means more of the other.

Don't believe me? Consider for a moment what it would be like to be homeless. Homeless people don't have to report to a job five days a week, do work they dislike, or take orders from a boss whom they hate.

They also have no bills to pay, no grass to mow, and no reason to dread the tax man. Their time is completely their own. Of course, they're also hungry every day, hot in the summer, cold in the winter, and very well may die early. And that doesn't even touch on their sense of meaning and purpose. It would seem that there's more to freedom than being completely unconstrained.

The reality is that, throughout our lives, we all accept more and more responsibilities precisely because of the freedom and opportunities they provide.

Yet, this fact somehow gets lost when it comes to children. Typically, these responsibilities even come with constraints on how we exercise the freedoms we already have, but it's not like they turn us into slaves.

Instead, the constraints themselves are often what enable us to pursue even greater freedom and opportunity.

As a teenager, driving a car is the ultimate freedom, until you take a corner too fast and get into your first fender-bender. As a student, getting assignments in on time and pulling all-nighters studying for exams certainly feels like a loss of freedom, but it opens the way for you to land a job that you're not going to hate doing when you're 40, and it gives you more opportunities for financial stability. Even marriage comes with new constraints as you suddenly have a partner to consider in everything you do and plan. Some people would call this a ball and chain, but a healthy marriage gives you a partner to enjoy life with, greater economic prosperity, and a stable relationship to start a family.

Becoming a Father is the Same

Becoming a father is a lot of responsibility that'll place constraints on your current life, but it opens up a whole new world of hard-to-quantify benefits, rewards, and opportunities to grow.

Of course, you don't fully grasp the benefits of parenthood until you've actually taken on the responsibility.

The *costs* on the other hand (expense, extra work, lack of sleep, etc) are more glaring, which makes avoiding the whole experience seem like the better option for many men. Talk about a leap of faith!

Fatherhood demands a massive shift in perspective, personal growth, and relational development for those who are brave enough to accept the challenge. If you take a closer look at the changes that happen after you become a dad, it all points to exchanging the more self-centered pursuits of your youth for more meaningful engagement with the world around you.

Not only does becoming a dad let you experience the world anew from the eyes of a toddler, but it makes everything you do, every choice you make, more meaningful.

Going to that pointless job you hate every day means more when it's teaching your children to overcome and persevere in the face of discouragement. The language you might carelessly use right now means more when you know your three-year-old is listening intently so he can be just like Daddy. How you look at, talk about, and treat women means more when you know it will play a bigger role than anything else in how your daughter views herself and what she ultimately ends up looking for in a man.

There's also the fact that these little people love you unconditionally, and in return, you yourself get the opportunity to learn selfless giving.

Having a child will show you where you're weak, immature, and selfish more than any other experience, and it'll give you a powerful reason to become a better person. And while kids are completely dependent on you initially, you get to be the coach and teacher who helps them to become independent men and women with talents, dreams, and achievements of their own. There is no more meaningful undertaking that most people will ever pursue.

Is all this supposed to come naturally? Yes, it's the only way. Some things can only be learned through experience.

It's also worth mentioning that fatherhood changes your interests and what matters to you just like any other major transition in life.

It's like going from high school to college or entering the world of work for the first time. Yes, you might be exchanging Friday night football games for a 40-hour work week, but you're also earning your independence and becoming self-sufficient, allowing you to discover more important and interesting pursuits. When that happens, it doesn't take long before your interest in high school sports fades into the background so you have time for those new passions you've discovered.

In some ways, shying away from the responsibility of a family because you think your life is already as good as it can get is kind of like Uncle Rico from Napoleon Dynamite clinging to his high school football days.

Don't get me wrong... high school football is great, and so is being content with where you're currently at in life, but there are more meaningful experiences that await you if you're just willing to let go of the past and shoulder a bit more responsibility.

Almost without exception, the most meaningful things in your life, and those that will make you grow the most, will be uncomfortable—maybe even outright painful—and involve sacrificial responsibility.

Becoming a dad fits into this category. But that's not to say that your social life, dreams, and hobbies are going to be permanently shipwrecked when you have a child.

Setting Expectations: Practical Tips

No, you won't be able to completely maintain your pre-child lifestyle any more than a married man can keep living like a bachelor, but the new constraints of being a father will be most severe when your child is really young.

And, with just a few adjustments, you'll eventually be able to do almost all of the same things you did before.

Tip #1: Spontaneity is Not Your Friend

For instance, spontaneity doesn't work when you have small kids because everything involving them takes careful planning. If they accompany you anywhere, you're going to have to factor in their schedule and routine, or the trip could become a nightmare. Luckily, it gets easier as they get older.

Sometimes you may need to arrange a babysitter or ask family to help out now and then, just to ease the load and free up some quality time for you and your partner. There are other adjustments you can make, too, like settling for a movie night at home after putting the kids to bed instead of going to the theater. You'll also find yourself spending more time hanging out at your house or friends' houses as opposed to bars or clubs.

Tip #2: Be Prepared for Some of Your Friends to Change

Some of your friends are going to change, too. The fact is, a lot of friends don't move with you when you transition from one phase of life to the next.

How many friends do you still have from your last job? College? High school? Overall, it may be difficult relating to friends who don't have kids. I've said it before; your really good friends are going to be around regardless, sneaking your kids candy when you're not looking. The rest may fall away, but that's to be expected.

My best friend is 12 years older than me, was married several years before me, and became a dad eight years before our first child was born. But we remained close friends throughout that time because we valued our friendship enough to maintain it, even when we were at very different points in our lives. If you and your partner don't feel like you have the time to stay connected with your friends, alternate baby duty on the weekends or evenings to give each other a break.

Tip #3: Keep Traveling, but Take it More Slowly

Another area that'll require some adjustments is travel, but you don't need to put your travel plans on hold indefinitely as I had initially feared.

When our firstborn was only four months old, my wife and I traveled to Tunisia for two weeks. Before he turned one, we did road trips from Virginia to Iowa and Atlanta for friends' weddings. For our fifth anniversary, we took a 10-day vacation to France when he wasn't yet two years old, and our second was only about six months old. Obviously, travel with toddlers is quite possible; it just requires a slower pace and a bit more planning.

Tip #4: Teach Your Kids Table Manners at Home

When it comes to eating out, there's no reason why this should screech to a grinding halt either.

We didn't change anything about our eating out routine, not even with four kids. As it is, babies mostly sleep in their car seats for the first six months of their lives, and once they become more active you can teach them how to behave at the table just by making them sit down for family dinners at home.

Tip #5: Don't Resign Yourself to Developing "Dad Bod"

Barring the initial few months after your baby is born, there's no need for you to put your workout routine on hold. The truth is, you should stay in good shape, physically and mentally, both for your baby and your partner.

If this is something you're concerned about, check for child-care options at your gym and turn gym-time into a date with your partner. If you're really that strapped for free time, you can even work out at home and include your baby in your exercise routine allowing you to bond and stay active at the same time.[2]

Fatherhood does come with a lot of added responsibility and some new constraints on life, but if you're afraid of losing your freedom, know this: your fears are probably exaggerated.

Not only will you be able to keep enjoying most of the things that are important to you, but you'll probably find that your kids will actually *enhance* all of those experiences. If you still don't feel "ready" to be a dad, I'll let you in on a secret.

You're never going to… not until you become one!

As for me, it turns out that having kids didn't mean that I had to give up those dreams I was scared of losing after all. Instead, sharing them with my kids has made them both more meaningful and more enjoyable than they would have been otherwise.

We did end up buying my grandparents' house—about two years ago—which means my kids will be the fourth generation in our family to live there. And, while we don't travel as much as we might otherwise, as I write this, I'm sitting in a hotel in Panama where we're taking a family vacation... an experience made all the richer when witnessed through the eyes of a five-year-old!

PART IV

HELPLESSNESS

10

MISCARRIAGE & HEALTH COMPLICATIONS – EVERY REASON FOR HOPE, NOT FEAR

I recently caught up with a friend whom I used to work with. He told me that his wife was pregnant, expecting their sixth child.

"Congrats.... That's wonderful!" I replied, remembering that he was adamant five years ago that they were done having kids. The news definitely took me by surprise.

It turns out he was surprised by it, too. "Yeah, thanks," he replied halfheartedly and then started to share. "I can't believe it happened. We're always careful. It was just that one time..." His voice trailed off.

I attempted to bring the conversation back on course. "Well, I'm happy for you. Another little one. That's exciting!"

"I should be happy. You know how I love kids," he responded. "It's just that my wife will turn 45 before the baby's born, and the doctors are treating this as a very high-risk pregnancy given her age and a few other factors. She's always delivered naturally, but the doctors are making sure she's prepared to have a C-Section, if needed, and she's getting all these extra tests.

"We're still in the first trimester, and I'm worried we'll have a miscarriage or that there'll be birth complications. I'm also worried because the chances of birth defects at this age are much higher than with our other kids.

"I know it might sound bad," he admitted, "but I just can't let myself get too excited until the baby is actually born."

The Risks are Probably Lower Than You Realize

Plenty of dads—even new dads whose partners aren't in their mid-forties—can relate to what my friend was feeling. Concerns about your baby's health and your partner's safety are only natural, even when a pregnancy is not high-risk, but these fears can be downright paralyzing for some dads.

Ten to 20% of pregnancies end in miscarriage [1] and around 80% of those happen in the first trimester. A lot of expectant fathers hear that and start bracing for disappointment.

But here's the thing; those statistics don't tell the whole story.

What you're less likely to have heard is that between 50 and 75% of miscarriages occur before ever getting a positive result on a pregnancy test.

By six weeks, the risk of miscarriage drops to just 5%, assuming your baby has a confirmed heartbeat, and by the time you get to 20 weeks, the chances are less than 1%.[2] Once a pregnancy reaches the 20-week mark, losing a baby isn't considered a miscarriage anymore but a stillbirth. And the chances of this decrease week by week, from 0.6% - 0.03%.[3]

So, yes, pregnancy loss does impact 1 in 5 couples, but many of them will never even know it.

The fact is that your partner's chances of carrying your baby full term are very good by the time you even realize she's pregnant.

Not knowing about a loss doesn't make it less of a tragedy—we're talking about human life after all—but it does mean that most couples have no reason to let themselves be controlled by fear of miscarriage by the time they hear the good news.

If the Unthinkable Happens

But what if your partner's pregnancy is at higher risk? Or what if <u>your</u> child ends up being one of the 0.03%?

The statistics don't matter in those cases.

But, even in those worst-case scenarios, trying not to become emotionally involved to 'protect' yourself, or letting your worries steal your joy doesn't help. While they are natural responses, they are not helpful responses.

While I'm very thankful that we've never had a miscarriage (at least to our knowledge), we're close with several couples who have. And they've each responded differently to their loss. For some, it was heart-wrenching. Others were able to move on more easily.

For those whom the pain and loss hit the hardest, their grieving came, regardless of how emotionally involved or joyful they were beforehand.

In no way do I judge my friend or others, who try to protect themselves from the disappointment and pain of a potential miscarriage. It's just that celebrating your child's life is a better way of dealing with his death, whether he passes away after 90 days in the womb or after 90 years on earth.

Life is a miracle, and each baby—born or unborn—has value no matter how long or short her life may be. Even if she lives for just a few months in the womb, she will be cared for there, nurtured by her mom, and loved by you both. That's a life worth celebrating.

Of course, it's not just the feeling of personal loss or even the awkward interactions with family, friends, and coworkers that some people are concerned about when it comes to miscarriage.

When you lose a baby, it can be tempting for a couple— and moms in particular—to blame themselves (or each other) and wonder if they did something to cause the miscarriage. But that's uncalled for.

About 60% of miscarriages are due to genetic issues, which means the unborn baby just wasn't developing properly.[4] More than half of miscarriages are caused by either missing or extra chromosomes caused by biological factors <u>not</u> inherited from parents.[5]

Even if you do everything right, there's nothing that either of you can do, or not do, to stop a miscarriage when there are problems with the unborn baby's DNA. Don't give in to guilt; this is nobody's fault.

Another common worry about miscarriage is that if a woman has one miscarriage, she's doomed to have more. Thankfully, that's completely false. Only 1 percent of women have recurrent miscarriages.[6]

And even with stillbirths, only about 60% have an identifiable cause—the most common being an issue with the placenta or the umbilical cord. Stillbirths can also be caused by birth defects or underlying medical conditions in the mother, like high blood pressure, diabetes, Lupus, or a severe infection.

Poor lifestyle choices also raise the risk of stillbirth, but that's pretty much the only cause you and your partner have control over.

So as long as your partner is eating healthily, avoiding harmful substances like alcohol and nicotine, cutting down on coffee, taking multivitamins, and generally taking care of herself, you're doing all you can to keep your baby safe in the womb.[7]

Some men are more worried about their partner not surviving the birth.

So, let me first say that even with a high-risk pregnancy, the chances of a woman dying during childbirth are extremely slim in developed countries where the latest medical technology is available.

In the US each year, less than 1 in 5,000 women (about 700 total throughout the country) die as a result of pregnancy or delivery complications. It's completely different from a few generations ago when childbirth was a high-risk endeavor. [8]

Unless your partner has an extremely high-risk pregnancy, she's got a greater risk of dying from constipation, which causes more deaths in the US each year than childbirth![9]

And a Word on Birth Defects and Prenatal Testing

Of course, miscarriage and complications during delivery aren't the only things that might be on your mind. There are also plenty of dads, similar to my friend, who are concerned that their kid might have a birth defect or some other serious health issue.

What father wouldn't be floored by the news that the baby he's eagerly anticipated for nine months has come into the world unhealthy and suffering from a lifelong condition that requires a lot more time, emotional support, physical care, and energy than he initially expected?

But then again, most babies are born healthy, with less than 3% of babies born in the US having a birth defect ranging from mild to severe.[10]

Generally, this isn't something that you should be losing sleep over.

The most common causes of birth defects are genetic abnormalities, some of which first-trimester prenatal screening can pick up. While your care provider will always recommend a prenatal test, most will only recommend further screening if there is a probability of genetic disorders that could affect both your baby and partner's health.[11]

Still, one caution when it comes to prenatal testing... you should probably avoid invasive diagnostic tests like amniocentesis or chorionic villus sampling. Sure, they may be more accurate than screening, but they increase the risk of miscarriage unnecessarily.

Amniocentesis is where a doctor uses a needle to take a sample of the fluid that surrounds your baby, and chorionic villus sampling is where the doctor guides a thin tube through the cervix or inserts a needle into the uterus to remove a sample of chorionic villus cells from the placenta.

The risk of this testing causing a miscarriage in the second trimester is about 0.1-0.3%, and even higher if done before 15 weeks of pregnancy. [12] Despite how small those odds are, it's just not worth it for an optional test that doesn't help protect your baby anyway.

While I think standard, non-invasive prenatal tests are valuable, you still need to know how to interpret the findings. A 'positive' test result doesn't necessarily mean your baby's going to be born with a defect. So, do your own research rather than blindly trusting your doctor or assuming the worst outcome.

Three of our four kids were diagnosed with something 'wrong' with them before birth, from missing a kidney to having a brain cyst to having a heart defect. Doctors referred us to medical specialists for each of these 'conditions'.

After birth, the pediatric nephrologist said our first son's one kidney had compensated and was performing as well as two, which is apparently quite common for babies born with one kidney. After 20 weeks, our second son's brain cysts resolved on their own, which is also apparently quite common. And after we researched the possible septal defect (i.e. hole in the heart) with our youngest daughter, we found out it was too small to have any noticeable effect and would likely close up on its own before birth.

Based on our research, we opted against getting an echocardiogram while pregnant, yet requested our child's circulation be tested after birth, and sure enough, she was healthy.

While my wife and I had a lot of questions with each prognosis, we did our own research so we had the whole picture, focused on the practical things we could do to mitigate the risks, and made a conscious decision to combat the fear.

Better to Have Loved and Lost

Of course, sometimes the outcome still turns out to be bleak.

Grief is to be expected when you find out your baby will be born with health issues. As a dad, you want to protect your child from harm and suffering. But don't fall into the trap of thinking that certain health conditions diminish the value of your child's life.

While they may make life harder, even the most chronic health conditions and disabilities don't need to stand in the way of children living happy, fulfilled lives. Your unconditional love is a powerful antidote to any health problems your kid may face.

Your baby asks for nothing else except to look into your eyes, to see your love, and to know that you're there for him.

Although the odds are against it, we all know couples who have experienced miscarriages or whose children had health complications.

If you happen to be one of those dads, as you and your partner grieve, you may grieve differently. Just make sure that you don't isolate yourself from one another or blame each other.

There's also no time limit to the healing process, and it may help to talk to a grief counselor or a religious or spiritual leader or a support group to help you through it.

For the dads who are looking forward to fatherhood and hoping their family will not fall into a low probability nightmare, don't worry about the risks of miscarriage, stillbirth, and birth defects.

Instead, focus on the positive things you can do to help your partner reduce these risks.

First and foremost, this means helping your partner establish and maintain healthy habits.

For example, smoking, alcohol, and recreational drugs are obviously off-limits for pregnant moms because they'll wreak havoc on your baby's development. But, if your partner has any of those habits, it's easier for her to abstain if you do so, too. The odds are actually six times better for couples who quit smoking together than for people who try to quit on their own.[13]

That principle also holds true for other important habits, like eating healthily and exercising—yes, that's good for pregnant moms, too, so long as it doesn't get her body temperature up too high.

Remember you and your partner are in this together, so whatever affects the one, affects the other, which in turn affects your baby.

Most importantly, replace the worry of loss with a celebration of what you do have.

In the words of the poet Alfred Lord Tennyson, 'Tis better to have loved and lost, Than never to have loved at all."[14]

Tennyson captured half the equation. The other half I'd say is from the baby's perspective... that it's better to *have been loved* and lost than never to **have been** at all.

Regardless of what happens in the future, your baby is already living a meaningful life and being loved. That is worth celebrating.

11

EVIL, PAIN, AND SUFFERING – IS IT RIGHT TO BRING A CHILD INTO THIS WORLD?

I n 2014, my wife and I made the worst financial decision of our lives.

The stock market had been on a tear for longer than most bull markets since the 1870s.[1] Real estate prices where we were living were up 10-20% above their 2007 highs, even though they'd lost half their value during the 2008 mortgage crisis. But I came of age during that crisis and witnessed the S&P 500 lose well over half of its value over the course of five months, so I knew how this kind of irrational frenzy would end.

Everything was a bubble on the verge of bursting. Another crash was imminent, and we knew it! So, what did we do? We pulled our money out of the market and sat on cash, waiting for a 'better' time to invest.

But that 'imminent' crash didn't happen for another six years. From mid-2014 to early 2020, the S&P 500 index rose from about 2000 to a high of 3397. That's almost a 70% increase, which we missed because we had 'protected' our money by sitting on cash.

Eventually, that crash we had envisioned did happen, but the S&P 500 never went below 2174—about 9% *above* where the market was when we pulled our money out six years earlier. Ironically, our extreme response, which was intended to avoid all the suffering we *knew* was coming, cost us more than the catastrophe itself would've.

Blinded by the potential loss of our retirement savings, we fled to the 'safety' of cash and suffered the much greater loss of a squandered opportunity.

A Generation Driven by Fear

The moral of my story is that decisions based on fear are almost always bad decisions.

We make our best choices not when we're running from something bad but when we're chasing something better. When we let our fears dominate us, we tend to make reckless, impulsive, and foolish decisions. This often starts by exaggerating the threat, which gives your fear hold over you and your actions and will ultimately cost you both your dignity and your chance for a better future.

Yet, fear is exactly what drives a lot of our generation's choices, including whether or not to have kids.

Just a few months ago, one of my wife's coworkers remarked that he and his fiancé would like to have kids, but they don't think it'd be responsible with "all that's going on in the world right now." What an ironic statement from someone living in the most prosperous era in world history, in the most socially mobile country in the world, with a job that places him firmly in the top 1% of income earners globally and the top 15% of Americans.

It's interesting that this dismal outlook seems to be most common among us Millennials and subsequent generations—people who've arguably grown up with the least deprivation of any generation in our country's history.

It's as if the wealth and ease of living in the US have produced an expectation that life will be easy. And when life is harder or more 'unfair' than we think it should be, our world is turned upside down. It's as if people interpret everything mentioned on the news or posted to Facebook as an existential threat.

This apocalyptic view of the world is only made worse by our tech-connected society where we're accosted daily with 24-hour news cycles. We all know that the content of news headlines is designed for its emotionalism and scare-effect. Sensationalized stories about war, natural disasters, violent crime, political unrest, and famine are way punchier than the more mundane realities of daily life.

Then there are Facebook and Twitter—true WMDs (weapons of mass deception)—whose algorithms are fine-tuned to censor counter perspectives while spreading polarizing memes, warped opinions, and self-reinforcing political propaganda with maximum impact.

Constant exposure to these types of influences only deepens any feelings of anxiety and hopelessness you might already be struggling with. Studies prove that the more you watch and listen to negative stories, the more you 'catastrophize' or, put simply, 'make mountains out of molehills'.[2] It even exacerbates personal concerns you might already have that are totally unrelated to the news content and blows them out of proportion.

The statistics on anxiety and depression back up what I'm saying about our generation.

Diagnosable anxiety disorders are becoming increasingly prevalent, especially among Millennials, with many people suffering from generalized anxiety disorder—a condition characterized by excessive worry and an unrealistic view of problems.[3] Interestingly enough, this disorder is more than three times as prevalent in high-income countries as it is in low-income countries, and it manifests most in the US.[4]

The persistent fear-mongering we're subjected to about the state of the world, economy, politics, and culture has collided with our societal expectations of ease. It's made our generation emotionally fragile and prone to exaggerate the threats we face.

Unplugging from the Matrix

To inoculate yourself against these influences, the first thing you need to do is stop reading the New York Times, turn off Fox News, and uninstall your Facebook app.

There was a time when I considered such advice irresponsible because I thought everybody had a duty to be 'informed'. Then, in 2013, I quit reading the news altogether. My stress levels plummeted, and I was shocked by how much my views changed when I started relying more on my own reasoning, research, and logic than my usual dose of daily 'programming'.

Now, I find the idea that news keeps you informed quite laughable, and that's not just my opinion. A recent survey of 92,000 people across 46 countries found that the US ranks dead last in people's trust in the media—at 29%—behind Nigeria, Bulgaria, and Turkey.[5]

This first step will do wonders to insulate you from whatever fear-porn happens to be in vogue, but it's not enough by itself.

You must also specifically seek out counter perspectives to the views that you do hold… not straw man caricatures, but the best-reasoned arguments you can find. Seriously, go look for that information; don't just wait to stumble upon it at your usual watering hole. Until you've worked as hard to disprove the beliefs that feed your fears as you have to fortify them, your doomsday convictions are unjustified.

And here's an additional caution: don't feel like your beliefs are more valid because you're in the majority. The more prominent your views are and the more loudly people in your own camp are shouting that the science is 'settled', the more vigorously you should dig to find honest arguments against them.

Why? Because censorship is more prominent than you think, and you're least likely to see it when your views are in the majority. Not only do most people's primary sources of information, like Facebook and Twitter, actively militate against the open exchange of ideas by censoring what these companies disagree with, but their algorithms create an echo chamber that reinforces groupthink, encourages polarization, and traps people in their fears.

Unless you're arrogant enough to believe that you have perfect knowledge and dumb enough to think Mark Zuckerberg is a neutral third party, it's vital that you actively seek out informed counter perspectives.

If you unplug from mass media and honestly seek out counter perspectives to what you're afraid of, I can virtually guarantee that 1) you'll realize that most issues are not nearly as hopeless as they're portrayed to be, and 2) not all of your fears are rational.

Kids Need 'Wind'

Failing to break this vicious cycle of hysteria and over-reaction makes us much more likely to run from our fears than to face them.

This is why some people, who are worried about what the world *may* become, choose not to have kids. They wrongly presume that kids have no place in the gloomy future they predict, but it's a false assumption that kids cannot thrive when exposed to uncomfortable, harmful, or even evil conditions.

A few years ago, scientists trying to prepare for the exploration of Mars created a biodome—a closed ecosystem that contained everything needed for life to flourish.

Devoid of all the deprivations and stresses that they would normally experience in nature, the trees and plants inside thrived. But, over time, the tiny saplings grew into large trees and began to die for no apparent reason. Eventually, every tree in the biodome cracked under its own weight and crashed to the ground.

Scientists eventually discovered that the trees had died because they grew in an environment without wind. Wind blows against trees, forcing them to sway and tremble. But it also forces the wood fibers that face the wind to grow strong and resilient so they won't be toppled. While scientists intended to create the 'perfect' environment for trees, they had instead destroyed them by removing every source of adversity and hardship from their lives.[6]

Our generation is a lot like those trees... so sheltered from adversity and flush with opportunity that we can't bear the weight of our own existence. Instead, we topple when faced with the slightest headwind.

Unlike the scientists, however, we've learned the wrong lessons from our fragile condition. Instead of embracing hardship, learning to overcome it, and teaching those same lessons to our kids, we try to build better domes to shelter them, or we just give up on planting trees altogether.

Kids need 'wind'. Not only is it impossible to shelter them from it, it's also reckless to try. We don't have to look far to see the crippling effects of being too sheltered from the difficulties of this world. They're obvious in children of overprotective parents—'helicopter parents'.

These parents keep their kids in a perpetual state of dependence by doing everything for them, which teaches learned helplessness and prevents them from acquiring vital life skills. Their children are denied the chance to prove their competence and take responsibility for themselves at an early age, predisposing them to depression, anxiety, and indecision. A lack of self-confidence and self-worth is likely to stalk them for the rest of their lives because the unintended message they've received throughout childhood is that they're not capable enough to face their problems, so they should run from them.

Childhood development expert, Lenore Skenazy, sums it up best: *"All the fear in the world doesn't prevent death - it prevents life."*[7] Not only is it healthy to face your fears, but it's also essential that you do so or they'll dominate you, costing you both your dignity and your future.

Charge Through the Darkness

My favorite movies are the "Lord of the Rings" trilogy, based on J. R. R. Tolkien's fantasy novels, which are set in Middle-Earth.

The story revolves around Frodo, who lives a quiet and peaceful life in the Shire, until he discovers the One Ring, which the Dark Lord Sauron created to control all the kingdoms of Middle-Earth. Frodo is forced to abandon his idyllic Shire as he and his companions undertake a perilous journey to destroy the ring. In his quest to conquer the last remaining strongholds of justice and good, Sauron searches for Frodo and the ring while his armies ravage Middle-Earth and leave a sea of destruction in their wake.

There's one scene where Frodo is speaking to his wise old friend Gandalf—a wizard guiding him on his journey—when he laments, "I wish the ring had never come to me. I wish none of this had happened."

Gandalf's response is penetrating. "So do all who live to see such times, but that's not for them to decide. All we have to decide is what to do with the time that is given us. There are forces at work in this world besides the will of evil."

It's not as if every fear that dominates people is imaginary.

In fact, most people's fears—like my fear of a stock market crash in 2014—have at least some basis in reality, even if they are exaggerated. But sometimes, even when we've purged our lives of hysterical voices and sought out the counter perspectives that might debunk our fears, we're still left staring down the devil.

We may even find that reality is worse than we initially suspected. The world may feel more like Middle-Earth —with evil clamoring up the walls of the last remaining strongholds—than the 'Shire' that we've come to expect from our upbringing.

In times like these, simply turning off the news and returning to reality isn't enough, but we don't have to carry these heavy burdens on our shoulders as hapless victims. We don't have to resign ourselves to whatever gloomy fate we fear, and we don't have to abandon our hopes and dreams for the future or make reckless decisions that cost us more than the fears we're running from.

What are you trying so hard to protect your future children from that you would think it is better for them never to exist rather than face those fears?

Is it crushing poverty? Then learn new skills, change where you live, and get a different job. Are you scared of what your kids will (or won't) be taught in school? Then home school or move to a better area, and make sure you're more attentive to your child's education than his teacher is. How about unjust discrimination? Then live with such a commendable character and competence that you tear down others' stereotypes and heap burning coals of guilt on the heads of your oppressors. Do you see cancel culture becoming more brazen and government becoming more oppressive? Then resolve to always speak the truth, and refuse to be silenced or participate in the lies—after all, "speaking the truth in times of universal deceit is a revolutionary act."[8]

My point is not to minimize any of these concerns because they're all valid. And I'm not saying any of this is easy, but I am saying that there are no circumstances in this life—regardless of how painful, hopeless, or final they may seem—that are completely irredeemable. Even if our actions cannot free us from suffering, we can choose to suffer well. There is always a choice to be made—something better to run toward

—even if it means charging through the darkness to do so.

However, this takes courage. It also means taking ownership of your situation, even if you didn't create it and you feel like it's out of your control.

The first and only North Korean I've ever met is my wife's stepdad. He was born in North Korea, shortly before the Korean War, to a well-connected family. His family knew when the Communists took power that the stakes were high and that the changes would come quickly: loss of their freedoms, confiscation of their property, and likely execution or torture, unless they betrayed their convictions and pledged allegiance to the new regime.

So they fled North Korea and made plans to come to America, but the journey was long and the costs were high. They left behind extended family, never to see them again. And, because they had to abandon their land and other possessions, they were broke.

For seven years, they lived in poverty in a South Korean ghetto. Eventually, they saved enough money and were able to get a visa and immigrate to the United States. But then they had to start over... again... with nothing.

Given the chances of failure, the high costs, and the danger of fleeing, it would've been easy for them to rationalize staying in North Korea, abandoning their beliefs, and groveling before the Communists in servile fear. Many people did. His family may have even kept their lives, their land, and some of their freedoms.

Even after they fled, they could've languished in that ghetto for the rest of their lives where they were at least able to speak the language and enjoy personal freedoms, but they didn't.

They didn't allow their fears to paralyze them into accepting life under tyranny or to chase them into a life of poverty. Instead, they set their eyes upon a better future—in America—and ran toward it, even though it meant running through the darkness.

It didn't matter that the threat was beyond their control. It didn't matter that the entire situation was unjust, or that running toward something better was going to cost them everything except their lives, at least in the short term.

Honestly, I can hardly think of a more hopeless situation, as an individual or as a parent, than the one his family found themselves in. Yet, by taking responsibility for their circumstances, they improved them against all odds.

Whatever circumstances you find yourself in, understand that they're probably not as dire as you think. But even if they are, you must take responsibility for changing them. Don't passively become a victim and allow your fears to dominate you. Don't run from pain, hardship, and work. Embrace the challenge... it makes you stronger. It will make your children stronger. And it might even make the world a better place.

PART V

FAILURE

FAMILY DYSFUNCTION – BREAKING THE "FIVE-GENERATION RULE"

W hat about yourself do you want to pass down to your kids and their kids?

A dad's brokenness has life-long effects on his kids, and many new dads who've grown up with dysfunctional fathers have valid concerns about continuing that destructive cycle with their own kids.

Nearly all of the social issues in America today can be traced back to kids growing up without a dad, according to some pretty bleak stats from the U.S. Census Bureau.[1] One in four kids in America (that's 18.3 million kids) grow up without their biological dad or any other positive father figure in the home. There are 10 million single moms, as opposed to two million single dads in the US, and 92% of the parents in prison are dads. What's more, when moms are both primary caregiver and sole provider, their kids have a four times greater risk (47.6%) of living in poverty.

Kids growing up without a dad are more likely to be high school dropouts who have behavioral issues. They're 279% more likely to carry a gun and deal in illegal substances, so they're definitely at greater risk of committing a crime and going to prison. And the legacy lives on because the stats show that kids with absent dads are more likely to be absent dads themselves.

And what about the dads who are physically present in the home but are abusive to their partners and kids or addicted to drugs, alcohol, etc.?

Kids growing up in a toxic environment like that can't be expected to grow up unscathed either. How we raise our kids today will impact our future generations, for good or bad.

Meet the Jukes and the Edwards

There's a famous story about two families from the 1700s in the US. One family had descended from Jonathan Edwards and the other from Max Juke.[2]

John Edwards went to Yale at thirteen and later became the president of what is now Princeton University. He went on to become one of the most renowned theologians and preachers in America. Being a devoted husband and dad to 11 kids, John Edwards made a real effort to be available to all of them. He was smart, a hard worker, with a high moral compass.

As the story goes, Max Juke wasn't some kind of wicked person, but he wasn't wild about school and dropped out early. He didn't like working hard either. He preferred fishing, hunting, trapping animals, heavy drinking, and telling vulgar stories. Not one for putting down roots, he built himself a make-shift home on the banks of a river and married a like-minded woman. He fathered a lot of kids, many of them illegitimate.

About two centuries later, when 1,394 known descendants of John Edwards were traced, they found among his impressive descendants: three senators, a US vice president, three governors, three mayors, and 30 judges. Additionally, there were 65 professors, 13 college presidents, 100 lawyers, 80 public office-holders, 75 Army or Navy officers, 62 physicians, 100 clergymen, some missionaries, and some theological professors. His descendants were diligent, law-abiding citizens.

Of the 1,200 descendants of Max Juke they were able to trace, 300 had died prematurely, and 67 died of Syphilis. There were 150 criminals, of which seven were murderers, 60 thieves, and 140 were convicted of various other crimes. Of the women, 190 were prostitutes, of whom 50 were 'career' prostitutes, averaging 15 years in the trade, 280 were poverty-stricken, and another 440 wrecked their lives through alcoholism and other addictions.

People tended to get the results of the study on the Edwards and Juke families twisted: they thought it proved that poor parenting and deviant behavior are genetic, which they're not

The study does, however, provide insight into how a legacy of good or bad behavior can be reproduced and multiplied through generation after generation. Sociologists call it the 'five-generation rule'. This means that what you put into raising your kids will impact not only their lives but the next four generations after them.

As you can see, your decisions as a dad will have far-reaching effects on your kids, and many will be inclined to follow in your footsteps.

Even Monsters Can Change

Sometimes, the source of a man's brokenness doesn't result from his own poor decisions or bad character traits. Things happen, and accidents or certain illnesses can lead to debilitating psychological and mental conditions that affect your ability to make the kinds of good parenting choices we've been talking about in the rest of this book.

The movie, '*I Can Only Imagine*', is based on the true story of Bart Millard, lead singer of the band "Mercy Me", whose dad suffered a head injury when he got hit by a diesel truck while working as a traffic guard at a construction site.

Arthur Millard woke up from an eight-week coma, a completely different person. He went from a gentle, peace-loving man to a foul-mouthed, mean-tempered monster. Bart's parents divorced when he was three, and he lived with his mom until the 3rd grade, after which he and his older brother went to live with his dad.[3] His dad wasn't an alcoholic or drug addict, but his spurts of uncontrolled temper transformed him into a beast who took out his frustrations on Bart, his regular punching bag.

One day, his dad had beaten him so severely that he could hardly walk or go to school for days, his back purple and blue with dark welts all over. He'd been sobbing for hours in his room when his dad decided to 'shut him up' and barged in, turning on the light. Only then did Arthur Millard see the damage he'd done to his son's body, and he froze, shocked to his core.

For the first time in his life, Bart saw his dad reduced to tears, deeply ashamed and remorseful. The beatings stopped.

The story took another turn when Arthur Millard was diagnosed with pancreatic cancer at age 44. He looked to God for solace, and through his faith, he was able to deal with his brokenness. Bart chose to care for his dad during his treatments, developing the kind of relationship with him that he'd always wanted, right up until Arthur Millard died.

It is NOT true that people are doomed to repeat their parent's mistakes.

Bart's story demonstrates that it doesn't matter how severe the legacy is that you're carrying; you always have the power to break the cycle and plot your own course. Neglect, abuse, divorce, addiction, poverty, narcissism, can all stop with you if you're willing to take up that mantle.

In the end, despite the severe abuse, the final choice lay with Bart to forgive, and grab onto his dad's positive and beneficial character traits and leave that as a legacy for future generations.

Of course, this is equally relevant for those of us without the severe childhood trauma that Bart experienced. Even the best upbringing is going to produce its own baggage.

When I think back on my childhood, I realize how blessed I was to have been raised by my parents. But after having my own kids, I began to see behaviors I learned from childhood that I needed to work on.

Let's be honest, kids can be frustrating at times, but instead of me managing those frustrations well, my default reaction was explosive anger and shouting. I was never taught emotional intelligence—the ability to perceive, articulate, and manage what I'm feeling at any given time—and I didn't see it modeled well, either.

I hadn't learned constructive ways to recognize or manage anger and disappointment as a child. But that knowledge empowers me to change, and while I don't claim to have it down, I've taken responsibility for how I respond, instead of blaming my kids for 'making' me angry.

I want to preserve a close relationship with them, prevent them from being scarred by my immature responses, and teach them from an early age how to handle their own emotions so that the quick temper stops with me.

Understand Your Dysfunction

When we think of negative father figures, the go-to is always the absentee *deadbeat* dad, and while that's the most common example, it's not by any means the only archetype. There are also narcissists—arrogant, self-centered men who do what they want, regardless of how it damages their families' wellbeing. There are overly critical dads, the ones that you just can't ever please, no matter what you do. Then there's the dad who focuses all his attention on his kids but ignores his wife, treating her like she's the help.

Some dads focus on their careers and neglect to make time for their families, even when they are home. Physically present but emotionally unavailable and distant dads can lead to kids who feel an acute sense of abandonment that could follow them into adulthood. It can, in turn, result in 'clingy and needy' young women or men who can't relate to their partner's and kids' emotional needs for love and attention.

Lack of communication, low emotional intelligence, lacking a deeper understanding of themselves or others, an inability or fear of commitment, and a deep fear of abandonment are usually primary obstacles that people face when trying to form and maintain healthy relationships in adulthood.[4]

The last two fears are the most damaging and are usually triggered by dads who've walked out, disengaged (sometimes after a divorce), or died prematurely. Their kids may grow up to shy away from committed relationships and be unable to bond with their own kids, crippled by a fear of losing the people they love.

Some examples of bad fathering may seem pretty normal, even positive to people on the outside. That makes it difficult for a kid to articulate the missing quality in their father-child relationship, or even identify the unhealthy behavior and how it makes them feel.

There's a heart-breaking song, written in 1974 by American singer-songwriter Harry Chapin, called "*Cat's in the Cradle*". It's about a dad who's always too busy to spend time with his young son, blowing him off, offering vague promises to spend time with him, but never doing it. Fast forward to years later, and the roles have switched. The dad, at some point while his son is at college, starts trying to reach out to him, wanting to build the bond that he never had time for when his son was a child. But his son speaks to him only long enough to borrow his car keys, then blows him off.

Fast forward a few more years, and his son has moved away. Married with a fast-paced career and kids of his own, the demands of his life are too many for him to make time to see his dad. And after the dad's pleas to see his son and spend some time with him are rejected yet again, a realization hits him: the little boy who had always been pleading for quality time with him, who was so in awe of him that he vowed to be just like him when he grew up, had done just that!

The song is about how negative behaviors get passed down from a dad to his kid. But in this case, it's not like the dad was some delinquent, abusive addict, sitting in a bar or having affairs, but rather, he was out building his career to pay the bills and give his kids a decent life and future. He just put all that ahead of his relationship with his kid.

Sometimes, those are the destructive behaviors that don't stand out with big neon letters saying, *"Don't do this to your own kids one day!"* because they come from pretty reasonable, responsible parents.

They're the ones you could mistakenly think you should be emulating, the ones that elicit a defensive "I'm doing the best I can" type reaction when that nagging voice in your head tells you something's off in your family life.

Of course, the song misses the fact that you always have a choice about whether to repeat your parents' mistakes or to actively choose a better way.

As a first-time dad, the fact that you're worried about being a good, loving father and guiding your kids to become healthy, balanced teens and adolescents means that your head and heart are in the right place, and you're already on the way to being the dad your kids need.

If you're committed to strengthening your bond with your kids, start by examining your existing or past relationship with your dad. Whether it was good or bad, or non-existent, it can be the key to improving your bond and parenting techniques with your own children.

Breaking the Family Cycle: Practical Tips

Just because your dad wasn't a criminal (like the Jukes) and didn't beat you till you couldn't walk (like Bart Millard's dad), that doesn't mean you aren't carrying some seriously harmful baggage that shapes how you relate to your partner and kids. You must identify the negative cycles that need to be broken and strengthen the ones you want to carry forward to future generations.

The fact that you're reading this book is already a positive sign that, on a deeper subconscious level, you're aware of some problems that need fixing. But while you may be able to name a few, it's unlikely you'll have pegged all the destructive relationship patterns you're prone to emulating if you grew up in a significantly dysfunctional family.

Tip #1: Become Self-Aware

We already covered that it starts with a decision to change, but it's impossible to change what you don't know. So, next, you'll need to become aware of repeated destructive patterns in your family history.

You'll get there by asking yourself the right questions, and a professional or even an emotionally healthy, stable person in your life can help you find out what those are.

Questions that you could ask yourself, to dig deeper and get to the crux of unhealthy interactions and behaviors, could include:

- What do I believe about myself and others that makes me think and act the way I do?
- How would I describe myself right now? Are my behavior, actions, and reactions leading towards a healthy, positive legacy for my children?
- How do I treat my partner and other women? Do I value and respect them as my equals?

- What assumptions, myths, and societal stereotyping are preventing me from being a supportive partner and the father my children would want in their lives?
- What wrong perceptions am I subconsciously clinging to from childhood about what a 'responsible and caring' father looks like?

Tip #2: Observe Others with Intent

Interact with other families you're close to, those who seem to model healthy relationships. And, when you do… purposely observe.

Check out how they deal with situations compared to how your family would've handled similar matters. Look out for positive things they do that make you 'uncomfortable', that 'would never happen' in your house. It may be things like open, confident communication about sensitive topics, or even a weird sense of calm in a crisis. Then, consider whether their way of doing things may be healthier than yours. If the answer is yes, try to work out what makes them different.

Look, this exercise might even fail because you're either surrounded by dysfunctional families or you could have a block that prevents you from seeing past the 'weirdness'. That's fine; Google can be your friend. Do some research on unhealthy patterns common to dysfunctional families and look for similarities with your own.

It might be easier to start with the unhealthy behaviors you're already aware of in your family. From there, your research may uncover a bunch of them that you had no idea about.

Then, start making a list of all the unhealthy ways you've come to think about relationships and yourself, which have followed you through childhood into adulthood. Also, write down the unhealthy patterns you've unconsciously fallen into as a result.

Tip #3: Take Personal Responsibility

Once you've identified the dysfunctional behaviors in your life that need to change, take responsibility for them. Forget about 'blaming' your dad or his dad. Remember, you can't change the past, and this might seem unfair, but if your response is to let it destroy you, that's on you. Your painful childhood experiences are valid, but don't get stuck there, hiding behind them.

You can't change anybody else. You can only change your attitudes and behaviors. What's more, you're the only one who can because nobody can slay your demons for you, although you could probably benefit from some guidance and support along the way.

Tip #4: Forgive

If your dad left you emotionally wounded and scarred, I have some news you're not going to like.

Deciding to pursue a different path isn't enough. You have to forgive him. Author and blogger, Mark Manson, stated it best: *"To continue to hold our parents responsible for their negative influence on our lives is to return to the mindset of a child — a mindset where we feel entitled to have everything fixed for us and where we perceive the responsibility for our lives to reside outside of ourselves."*[5]

Forgiving your dad doesn't mean that you develop a sudden case of amnesia over your childhood or condone it in any way. It's a deliberate decision to release any resentment or anger that you may harbor against him.

Whether he deserves it is irrelevant.

You can't change him, but if you don't forgive him, you'll never be free of his dysfunctional legacy. As Manson explains it, *"True adulthood occurs when we realize that our parents didn't dig the hole that we find ourselves in today, but rather that they've been trying to climb out themselves their whole lives; that the abuser was once the abused. That the neglecter was once the neglected."*[6]

Tip #5: Reframe Your Thinking

Once you've recognized the dysfunction in your relationships and family, taken responsibility for changing your behavior, and forgiven your parents, it's time to let go of the past, to stop focusing on what you don't want to be and turn to the future. Focus on what you WANT to become.

Wait! But shouldn't focusing on avoiding negative behaviors automatically produce the desired effect? Wrong. Get this - research shows that our brains can't process the word, *'don't'.* [7]

When you were a kid, did your mom ever tell you not to eat a cookie before dinner? I bet all that you could think of from that moment on was the cookie. It's because your brain focuses on the subject at hand, so instead of telling it what *not* to do, it's better to tell it what *to* do. "Eat an apple" would have worked way better than "Don't eat that cookie'.

The same principle applies to changing your outlook and actions as a dad. Instead of resolving, "I *won't* neglect my family the way my dad did," you can declare, "I *will* make time for my partner and kids every day."

What I'm saying is you might start with that negative list that you created of all the things you resent about your dad or don't like about yourself. But then you'll have to transform it into a list of all the positive things you wish he would've done instead, and those are the actions that you should commit to doing.

If that's a limited list, look at qualities you admired in other dads, teachers, pastors, and neighbors, who inspired you while you were growing up. Which of those character traits do you wish you had? What actions do you need to take to develop them? And are you willing to do whatever it takes to get there?

13

FALLING SHORT – HOW NOT TO BE THE "PERFECT" DAD

S ooner or later, every man who's about to become a father has a moment of honest self-reflection and wonders whether he has what it takes to be a good dad. But some dads are paralyzed by the fear that they don't.

This fear of failure doesn't always come from a childhood filled with the type of obvious brokenness we covered in the last chapter. Many men just don't feel like they're 'ready' to be dads, and they experience a more generic (but no less crippling) sense of personal inadequacy and unpreparedness for the task ahead.

Both types of men are afraid of failing, but in different ways.

The first dad is convinced that he's broken and can't be fixed—that he *will do* everything wrong, just like his old man. The second dad simply feels like he *must do* everything right since raising a kid is a massive responsibility. The first man feels damned to play the devil, but the second feels like he's expected to be God. And who can do that?

The song *"Growing Up"* by rapper and hip-hop artist, Macklemore, is a really good example of this. He wrote the song while his partner was pregnant with their daughter, and it's all about how he wanted nothing more than to be a good dad but didn't feel ready and was afraid he'd mess things up. He said as much in a letter to his fans telling the story behind the song:

> *"[...] I think back to that night: praying on the floor at 2 am as Tricia went to the bathroom to take a pregnancy test I'd just purchased from Walgreens. I was scared. Scared to start working on new music. Scared of trying again and failing. Scared of the process of staring at myself through a page and seeing something that I wasn't proud of. Someone that I didn't like. Someone that wasn't ready to be a dad."*[1]

Even the name of the song suggests that he felt like he was still growing up himself and couldn't possibly raise a kid—a sentiment echoed throughout the song's lyrics.

There are a lot of reasons why new dads don't feel up to the task. That's what this whole book is about. And, while you probably haven't experienced all of these fears yourself, chances are that at least a few of them feel familiar to you.

After all, there seems to be increasing pressure in our society to 'get it right'—whatever 'it' is.

Perfectionism's Ugly Offspring – Obsession & Avoidance

In our connected world, it's easy to fall into the trap of thinking you have to compete with airbrushed versions of other people's lives, whether it's wearing designer labels, driving luxury cars, or having your kid enrolled in violin class by age three.

This isn't just speculation, either. A recent study shows that perfectionism and social comparison have become a lot more common over the past few decades, especially among young people.[2]

Some people treat perfectionism like it's a good thing—almost like it belongs on their resume—but it's really never healthy.

Along with this increase in perfectionism, there's been a steady rise in anxiety, depression, and suicidal tendencies. [3]

It's no wonder that many new dads fear they won't measure up.

But, the ironic part about fearing that you'll fail as a dad is that it's often self-fulfilling. The pressure to be perfect when it comes to such a high-stakes responsibility often triggers two contradictory impulses: obsess or avoid.

On one hand, some dads respond to that fear of falling short by obsessing over their own and their kids' shortcomings in an effort to be the 'perfect', involved dad and raise 'perfect' kids.

The result: guilt-ridden, controlling fathers and stifled kids who stand a slim chance of developing their own personality, making their own decisions, or being able to solve their own problems.

My wife and I know a super-intelligent, high-performing businessman, who is so controlling that his kids—now in their 20s—still lack any observable sense of individuality or confidence.

We asked his 23-year-old daughter to babysit our kids one day while we did some work around the house. We couldn't believe that he was the one who decided whether or not she would accept the work. He was even the one who dropped her off at our house so that he could see for himself where his adult daughter, who could not yet drive, would be working for the day!

His daughter lacked the confidence to take initiative, constantly asking us for permission to do anything. Worse yet, she couldn't seem to stop herself from shushing our kids the entire day, even though we told her that we don't expect toddlers to be silent all the time.

I realized where that came from when her dad picked her up and boasted about how well his daughter "keeps kids quiet".

It was obvious that this dad demanded "perfection" of himself and his children. No doubt, he was the overly-involved father, who made sure his daughter always asked permission from him, so she wouldn't mess up.

But this obsession to attain such impossible standards ended up with the opposite effect, warping his role as a dad and crushing his daughter's personality to the point that she was a slave to her fear of making a "mistake."

On the other hand, there are plenty of men who respond to their fear of failing as a dad by avoiding the very thing they're scared of messing up.

Perhaps they doubt their ability to be good fathers, or perhaps they just don't feel like they're at a place in life where they're 'ready'—like Macklemore. Either way, their instinct is to retreat, since they don't know how to do it 'right'.

We have a good friend whose parents got divorced when she was a little girl. After a few years living with her mom who neglected her, her dad and grandparents got custody, and she went to live with them.

Not only did her dad's job in the construction industry demand long work hours, but he's introverted by nature and used to dealing with men, not teenage girls.

So, every night after work, he would disappear to the basement rather than spend time with his daughter.

At one point, she confided in her grandparents that it felt like he ignored her. She was surprised when they told her what her dad had shared with them. He loved her immensely. He simply didn't know how to relate to his daughter, and he was afraid to try and fail.

After all, what does a teenage girl want to talk about? The worlds of construction and middle school don't have a lot in common.

He wasn't sure what she expected of him as a dad, and whatever it was, he didn't think he had it in him. It was much easier to watch TV alone in his bedroom than to feel like he was falling flat on his face each time he tried to engage with his daughter.

Overcoming the Fear of Failure: Practical Tips

When it's not dealt with, the fear itself is often what will keep you from trying in the first place, like our friend's dad. Or, it can drive you to become an over-bearing helicopter parent, like our babysitter's dad.

Yes, your apprehensions about such a big life change are natural and normal, but you must move beyond them. Here are four key steps to overcoming your fear of failure and becoming an exceptional dad.

Tip #1: Strive for Excellence, Not Perfection

Perfectionism can fester unrecognized for a very long time because it often masquerades as a more positive trait like striving for excellence. And, while those two things might look similar on the outside, they're completely different on the inside.

People who pursue excellence set high standards and seek out challenges, achievement, and accomplishment for their own inherent value. Yet, true perfectionists are driven by their fear of failure, judgment, and rejection.

They don't just set unrealistically high standards; they have intensely negative reactions when they or their kids don't measure up to those ideals.

While they might wear their "high standards" like a badge of honor, the fact is that people who are able to give themselves grace and learn from their mistakes, rather than beating themselves up, will always have the upper hand.[4]

Tip #2: Avoid Dichotomous Thinking

Dichotomous thinking— seeing the world in black and white—is often the root of a new dad's fear of failure because he equates mistakes with failure, but they're not the same thing.

We all make mistakes as dads—sometimes really big ones—but that doesn't automatically make us failures.

Some psychologists call this mindset the "God/scum phenomenon". [5] Everybody, including the perfectionist himself, is either perfect or totally worthless when measured against his lofty expectations. There's no in-between.

This kind of all-or-nothing approach doesn't work well in any area of life, but it's especially damaging when it comes to relationships. Because there's no objective standard for 'success' and outcomes are never 100% under your own control, dichotomous thinking will always make you feel like your kids are failing you or you're failing your kids.

It'll also affect your happiness as a parent by causing increased stress. Constantly feeling like a failure makes it harder to adapt to fatherhood, makes it less enjoyable, and results in generally poor parenting. In some cases, it can even affect your level of commitment to being a dad as you start regretting having had kids in the first place.

Shifting your mindset won't just happen overnight, but it could be that becoming mindful of your own behavior, your self-talk, and interactions with others will be enough to start the transformation process.

However, if your fear of failing is noticeably affecting your mental well-being, your relationships, or other areas of your life, it's time to get professional help.

Tip #3: Reframe What 'Success' Means in Your Role as a Dad

This means replacing that dichotomous thinking with healthier beliefs that more accurately reflect reality, like these:

- **Failure is not final, nor is it damning.**
  Mistakes are isolated, temporary, and crucial
  for learning anything. It is possible to 'fail
  forward' by learning from your mistakes, and
  you'll be stronger for it. Just as you should
  allow your kids to make mistakes without you
  lashing out or taking control, allow yourself as
  a dad to make mistakes without beating
  yourself up and withdrawing.
- **Success is a direction, not a destination**, so
  celebrate every step of progress, even when
  your expected outcome isn't met. Your starting
  point and your finish line will look different
  from those of other dads, so don't compare
  yourself to them or judge yourself by anybody
  else's expectations... including your kids'.
  Instead, measure yourself today against who
  you were yesterday and draw confidence from
  even the tiniest step closer to those goals that
  you're working toward. Don't focus on the final
  outcomes, but rather take encouragement from
  putting in the effort and moving in the right
  direction, even in just a few areas.
- **Success is multi-dimensional.** At any given
  point, you're probably going to feel like you're
  failing as a dad in some areas, but don't lose
  sight of how well you're doing in others. The

reality is that you're never as good as you think you are, or as bad as you think you are.

Let me give you an example from my own life. As I've said before, patience is not one of my strengths. It never has been. I've always struggled to maintain my composure when I get frustrated, and kids can be very frustrating.

I know that about myself. After all these years, it's still an area where I need to grow, but it's only one aspect of my parenting. I also know that I'm very good at verbally affirming my kids, telling them I love them, showing them physical affection, and apologizing when I do fail, which leads me to my last point…

Tip #4: Apologize Often

Whether you've said or done something wrong to your partner or your kid—no matter how young—there's no more powerful way of fixing your relationships, demonstrating humility, and building trust.

You might feel like a hypocrite, apologizing for the same thing for what seems like the hundredth time, but you've still got to do it. It's an essential relational 'reset'. When you apologize, you take ownership of your mistake rather than covering it up, pretending it didn't happen, or sweeping it under the rug, hoping no one else thinks it's a big deal.

This shows both you and your kid that screwing up isn't the end of the world. Making yourself vulnerable teaches your children that love, acceptance, and self-worth aren't a result of being perfect or meeting expectations. We don't need to be perfect because there's grace for a humble spirit.

Your kids don't need a "perfect" dad. They just need you.

PART VI

FINANCIAL RUIN

14

MEDICAL BILLS – HOW TO CUT COSTS BY 80%

The health insurance system in the United States is both unique and convoluted. So, some of this information may not be directly relevant if you don't live here, but you still might be able to adapt these powerful strategies to your own situation. And, this chapter will certainly serve as inspiration for the power of thinking outside the box if you're worried about the medical costs associated with pregnancy.

More than $28,000. That's how much the medical costs were for our second son's birth from conception to delivery. And things didn't get any better with our daughter 19 months later. Her bill came in at just over $29,000.

Our first child's bill was in the same ball park, but I don't have the invoices to count up exactly what we spent. Here's the thing; every one of their births was a normal, healthy, complication-free delivery.

Yet, when our fourth kid was born a short time later, her birth only cost about $6,000. It would've been closer to $5,000 if we hadn't switched medical providers mid-pregnancy!

How's it possible for the same woman to receive more or less the same medical services, in the same state, two years *later*, and have it cost less than 20% as much?!

In essence, that's what this chapter is about... answering that question so that you and your partner can make smarter decisions about your baby's birth, without going broke or compromising the quality of your family's care.

Not being able to make ends meet is one of the top concerns that new dads have, and medical costs are among the biggest expenses you're going to face. Unfortunately, they're also the hardest to estimate ahead of time, because health insurance and medical billing are so opaque and convoluted, almost intentionally so.

Thankfully, my wife and I had decent insurance when we had each of our kids, so that covered a large portion of those jaw-dropping $28,000 and $29,000 invoices.

But it wouldn't have covered nearly as much as it did if we hadn't learned the powerful tactics that I'm about to share with you for evaluating and choosing the best insurance plans.

But what do you do if you don't have good insurance options to choose from? Many people don't.

I've got you covered… no pun intended.

A lot of people assume that having good insurance is the only way of managing pregnancy-related healthcare costs, which is simply false. In fact, as you'll soon learn, it may not even be the best way.

Our insurance played absolutely no role in lowering the bill for our youngest daughter's birth to just $6,000. There were no adjustments, no reimbursements… just a cash payment to the provider and a willingness on our part to stop following the herd.

So, whether it's using my strategies to maximize the value you get out of your health insurance, or finding ways to lower what you're billed in the first place, this chapter can help just about anybody save massive amounts of money on medical costs when expecting a baby.

Regardless of your circumstances, you and your partner have more control over these costs than you realize.

In fact, for many people, taking action on what I'm about to teach you will probably *slash your total medical expenses by 50% or more*. And I'm not just talking about the year that you have a baby... but on an ongoing basis.

I'm also going to show you how some people can even make money off of their health insurance. Yeah, you read that right.

This isn't possible for everybody, because it depends on what benefits your employer offers as well as a few other details, but my wife and I have done this successfully for a number of years.

A Completely Different Approach

Here's the catch. You don't get these kinds of results by doing what everybody else is doing... by listening to conventional "wisdom". These kinds of rewards are reserved for those people who are willing to put in the hard work of learning and making a different choice than everybody else—not a worse choice, not even a riskier choice, just a different one.

With our first baby, my wife and I pretty much did what everybody does.

My wife chose her OBGYN based on a friend's recommendation. She gave birth at the nearest hospital without realizing we even had the option of doing anything differently. We got whatever lab work was suggested by the doctor, without question, and we automatically used whatever specialist we were referred to for third-party services, like the standard 20-week anatomy ultrasound.

But, over the course of each pregnancy, we learned.

We learned not only that you can switch insurance plans when your baby is born, but also that the new plan usually provides coverage retroactively to the child's birth date. So, if you change plans immediately after your baby is born, the new plan ends up covering the vast majority of medical costs associated with the pregnancy—not the plan you actually had on the day junior came into this world.

We learned that the exact same anatomy ultrasound that we were charged $2,800 for by the specialist (to whom our OBGYN referred us for our first child) really only costs $250 at the radiology clinic two miles down the road, if you pay with cash.

We learned that the invoice from the hospital alone accounted for $19,000 of that $29,000 bill for our daughter. Mind you, this didn't include any actual care from a doctor or pediatrician; rather, it covered a room, a bed, a few over-priced supplies, some marginal cafeteria food, and the largely unnecessary checkups from nurses that kept my wife from getting any rest during the two days she was in the hospital.

We learned a lot. But, the most important thing we learned was the difference between doing something because it is what everybody else is doing and doing something because it is what's best for your family.

By the time we had our fourth child, we took a completely different approach.

Instead of signing up for whatever ultra-low-deductible, "Cadillac" health insurance plan our employers offered, we opted for a high-deductible plan with a health savings account (HSA) and low premiums. Instead of giving birth at our local hospital, my wife decided to try a birthing center within spitting distance of the hospital. Instead of seeing an OBGYN for prenatal care, the highly-skilled midwife at the birthing center did regular prenatal checkups. And, instead of blindly following whatever referrals we were given, we price-shopped for any third-party services we needed.

The difference? Thousands of dollars in savings and the least stressful delivery that my wife had out of all our kids.

How to Slash Your Medical Costs: Practical Tips

I can't detail all of the specific tricks and tactics that you can use to save money on your medical bills... there are far too many to cover in this chapter, and everybody's situation is a bit different. Instead, I want to focus on those couple of decisions where most people will get the most benefit.

The number of zeros you end up staring at on your medical bills after your baby is born will be overwhelmingly decided by two choices that you and your partner make: 1) What health insurance plan did you choose? and 2) Where did your partner give birth?

In the rest of this chapter, I'm going to share practical tips about how to save thousands of dollars on medical costs by making these decisions well.

Most of these tips revolve around choosing health insurance. Because everybody learns better with concrete examples, I'm going to give you real numbers to show you how powerful these strategies are, but my examples are based on two key assumptions:

- All of your family's pregnancy-related medical bills occur within the same year on your insurance plan.
- You will only use "in-network" healthcare providers.

Important Health Insurance Terms

In-Network: "In-network" healthcare providers are doctors, clinics, hospitals, etc, who've agreed to your insurance company's billing rates. If you go to an "out-of-network" provider, you'll have to cover more of the cost yourself. Some types of plans, like Health Management Organizations (HMOs), may not cover any of the costs for out-of- network services.

Deductible: A deductible is how much of the bills from the doctor you must pay before your insurance plan helps. Most plans have separate "individual" deductibles and a "family" deductible. Many plans also have higher (and sometimes completely separate) deductibles for services obtained "out-of-network". All of these deductibles reset every year, or every time you change insurance plans. Copays don't normally count toward your deductible.

Coinsurance: Coinsurance is the percentage of your bills that you'll still have to pay, even after you've met your deductible and insurance starts to help. Within a plan, this percentage is normally fairly standard from one type of service to another. For example, your coinsurance might be 10% for most types of service, but there are instances where your coinsurance obligation could be different from one type of service to the next (e.g. maternity vs emergency room visits). You have to check your plan to know for sure.

Copayment: A copayment ("copay") is a flat fee that some insurance plans make you pay for certain services every time you receive them. For example, you might have to pay $35 for every doctor's visit you have, or $15 for every prescription you get filled. Not all plans have copays.

Out-of-Pocket (OOP) Limits: OOP limits represent the most that you'll be expected to pay during a given year in the form of deductibles, copays, and coinsurance. Like deductibles, there are normally separate OOP limits for each individual as well as a "family OOP limit". There may also be separate OOP limits for in-network versus out-of-network services. After your OOP limit is reached, your plan should pick up all future expenses that are covered, until the next plan year.

Tip #1: Insurance Premiums Matter as Much as (or More Than) What Your Plan Covers

When you think about the medical costs of having a baby, what comes to mind? Delivering at the hospital, prenatal checkups, an ultrasound, blood tests, your partner's OBGYN... anything else?

A lot of people are so focused on how their insurance policy will cover the specific medical services they'll need, that they overlook what is often the biggest medical expense of all: insurance premiums.

Many people are terrified by the idea of going to the doctor and having to pay several thousand dollars out of their own pockets before insurance kicks in. So, it's logical when these folks expect a large medical expense that they can anticipate—like pregnancy—that they would opt to purchase a Cadillac insurance plan, with extremely low deductibles and coinsurance obligations, if they can afford it.

Sounds like they're "getting one over" on the insurance company, right? Wrong.

What they unfortunately don't realize, and can't easily figure out, is that the sky-high insurance premiums for Cadillac plans with those low deductibles will almost always leave them poorer than more affordable plans, even during years when they use a lot of medical services.

And it gets worse if you're somebody who holds this type of low-deductible plan year-in and year-out, because these high premiums hurt you the most in those years when you don't need as many medical services.

You see, insurance premiums are a guaranteed cost every year, whether you go to the doctor or not, whether your partner is pregnant or not.

Just because they're deducted from your paycheck before you ever see the money in your bank account doesn't change the fact that they're leaving you poorer at the end of the year.

But, minimizing your costs isn't always as simple as just choosing the plan with the lowest premiums. Some people do that without understanding why those premiums are so low. Then, when they go to the hospital, they find out that their plan has large copayments, terrifying deductibles, massive coinsurance obligations, and jaw-dropping "out-of-pocket" limits.

Most people don't have a clue how to figure out which plan is the best for them because it's complicated, so they use shortcuts (e.g. fear of large deductibles) to choose their policy, which virtually guarantees bad results.

Over these next few pages, I'm going to explain how you can choose an insurance policy that you're confident will give you the best care at the cheapest price.

Tip #2: Purchasing a Bad Insurance Policy Can Cost You More Than Having No Insurance

As part of my research for this book, I did an in-depth analysis of dozens of insurance plans from various employers and government-run insurance exchanges to see how much a couple having their first baby would have to pay.

For each plan, I factored in everything that would impact that couple's finances, including insurance premiums; out-of-pocket medical costs like copays, coinsurance, and deductibles; tax savings from paying premiums with pre-tax dollars; tax credits from government subsidies; tax savings from health savings accounts... everything.

I wanted to know how much poorer that couple would be at the end of the year after everything had been taken into account.

Some of what I found shocked me.

When faced with large medical bills, like childbirth, a lot of people just assume that <u>any</u> health insurance is better than <u>no</u> health insurance. After all, how could it not be better since they're paying some of your bills?

This is another of those mental shortcuts, which happens to be very wrong and can cost you thousands of dollars. And, yet again, a lot of it comes down to premiums.

Sure, almost any plan will provide some savings in overall out-of-pocket medical costs, but a particularly bad plan will end up costing you more in premiums than it saves you at the doctor's office.

Let me give you an example. I did my analysis on every single health insurance plan available to people living in my zip code that was listed on the government-run exchange healthcare.gov—the official site of the Affordable Care Act, which was rolled out under Obama in 2010.

Here's what you and your partner would've paid out of your own pockets if your insurance plan was billed

$29,000 (for mom and baby combined)—as was the case for me and my wife with our first daughter.

If you'd purchased the best performing plan on the exchange, you still would've been $22,530 poorer at the end of the year when every form of cost or incentive was taken into account. That wouldn't have saved you much of the cost, but $6,500 is certainly nothing to sneeze at.

But, this is where things get interesting. The worst performing plan on the exchange would have left you $33,323 poorer after everything was said and done. Yet, the childbirth itself only cost $29,000, so how is that?!

That plan would've cost you just over **$4,000 more** than if you had no insurance at all!

And that's a year when you really "got your money's worth" by actually using a lot of medical services. Imagine if you hadn't used any, but you'd still be on the hook for that plan's $17,216 in annual premiums every year!

As I said, much of this comes down to premiums, which most people ignore. So, yes, having some insurance plans can be worse than having no insurance at all.

Tip #3: Avoid Government-Run Insurance Exchanges Like the Plague

Now, the numbers I just gave you are for a couple with only one kid, who is purchasing these plans at full price. Admittedly, these exchanges really weren't designed for people who would have to purchase insurance on them at full price, but that still doesn't mean they're a good deal for people who are eligible for tax credits.

If that same couple in my example above had an annual combined income of $68,000—the average household income for Americans at the writing of this book—they'd qualify for a massive tax credit of $9,804 per year.

Even with this $10,000 subsidy, three of the 13 plans that were available for me to analyze on healthcare.gov would've cost that couple more than $20,000 out of their own pockets for a childbirth that cost $29,000.

Now, you may be tempted to think that's still not a bad deal because they saved $9,000.

Well, not exactly.

Insurance companies represent a lot of patients—all of whom are potential customers for healthcare providers —so they're able to negotiate with providers to get a large break in price. That's what it means for a doctor to be "in-network"; those doctors don't actually get paid the amount that they're billing.

When you pay for that company's insurance plan, you gain access to their network of doctors and lower prices for their services.

This price negotiation is possible because it only costs a hospital about 30% of what is billed in order to perform its services.[1]

How about for those without insurance? Well, most people who don't have insurance can't afford to just shell out $29,000 on the spot, so medical providers tend to also negotiate with cash-paying customers. If you're paying cash, you should always ask for a discount, and many providers will drop prices by as much as 30%, just because you asked.[2]

So, let's go back to the example at hand. That $29,000 price tag on childbirth is what your insurance would be billed before their negotiated adjustments. If you were to negotiate as a cash-paying customer, it would very likely be discounted to as little as $20,000.

Those insurance plans don't look so attractive any more, do they? The fact is that three out of the 13 plans I analyzed on that exchange would have still cost you as much as or more than paying cash to have your child...

and that's after factoring in almost $10,000 in tax credits to offset the premiums.

The worst plan would have cost you about $3,500 more than paying cash. Notably, that's the plan with the highest premiums.

Now, there are certainly some really bad employer-sponsored health insurance plans out there, but on government-run exchanges, bad plans are the norm.

If you have access to health insurance through your employer, it will almost always be your best option. It still may not be great, but it will probably be better than going to a government-run exchange. The reason for this is that most employers actually pay part of your premiums for you; you just don't see those payments as an employee.

There are some exceptions to this rule. For example, if your income is low enough, you may not have to pay anything at all for premiums if you go to a government exchange. So, in those cases, some of these plans could make sense, but know that plans like those will only really save you money if you have a catastrophic medical emergency that runs into the hundreds of thousands of dollars in cost.

As a general rule, government-run healthcare exchanges should be your absolute last resort.

Tip #4: It's Actually Possible to Make Money Off Your Health Insurance

Most people only think of health insurance as a way of saving money, so it really blows their minds when I teach them how to make money by purchasing health insurance.

Yeah, you read that right. In some situations, you can essentially get paid to buy health insurance... and not just a little bit of money either. I know it sounds absurd, but it's true.

Let me explain how this works.

If you've spent any time evaluating health insurance plans, you've probably come across a type of plan called a high-deductible health plan (HDHP).

For the most part, HDHPs work like other health insurance plans, but they tend to have much higher deductibles—hence the name. In many cases, these deductibles might be twice, three times, or even four times as high as otherwise-similar plans offered by your employer.

And, of course, you have to pay these deductibles before the insurance company will cover any of your bills. After that, HDHPs tend to have similar coinsurance requirements and OOP limits as other plans from the same provider.

A lot of people are scared of HDHPs, especially if they know they're going to have medical expenses—like having a baby. After all, why would you choose a plan with a high deductible when you <u>know</u> that you're going to max it out that year?

Surely, a low deductible plan would cost you less in the long run! Right?

Wrong.

Admittedly, the logic seems sound enough... until you actually run the numbers and calculate <u>all</u> of the costs associated with the plan, not just how it covers medical services.

So, we come back to my very first point: that premiums matter as much as (or more than) how your plan covers your family's medical care. You see, in return for that high deductible, HDHPs often (but not always) have substantially lower premiums than other plans from the same provider.

By way of example, let me compare two insurance plans offered by my wife's employer. One is a Cadillac plan with a really low $1,000 family deductible. Just the premiums for this plan would cost us $6,216 per year. Now, bear in mind that these premiums are <u>guaranteed expenses</u> that we would have to pay every year we were on the plan, even if we never saw a doctor or received any care.

By contrast, the plan that we purchased is an HDHP that costs only $3,000 per year in premiums and has a $4,000 family deductible. So, if we had another baby next week, we would need to stand the first $4,000 of cost out of our own pockets without any help from insurance, but that's only if we need to use that amount of medical services that year.

Most years, our family only needs standard preventative care (100% covered by most plans), which means we're saving $3,216 in premiums, just because we went with an HDHP over a more expensive, low-deductible plan. Over a five-year period, that adds up to more than $16,000 worth of savings from the premiums alone.

That still doesn't explain how we can make money off insurance, but the low premiums are just the tip of the iceberg.

HDHPs make you eligible to open a health savings account (HSA). This is a special bank account that lets you save money <u>without ever paying income tax</u> on it, as long as you only use the funds to pay for your family's medical expenses. And I'm not just talking about federal income tax either; most states don't tax HSA contributions.

The IRS adjusts how much money you can contribute to an HSA each year, but the tax savings from maxing out your HSA can amount to several thousand dollars a year, depending on your income tax rate. This year, maxing out our HSA should save us $1,812 just in taxes.

But it gets better.

Many companies, especially larger organizations, contribute money to their employees' HSAs when they opt for an HDHP. Of the three organizations that I've worked for before becoming an entrepreneur, every one of them has contributed funds to my HSA.

My wife's current employer does the same. In fact, they contribute $2,400 of un-taxable money into our HSA. Understand, this is $2,400 that she's getting paid every year, which we would not receive if we chose any of the other insurance plans they offer.

Now, let's do some math. I don't know whether you've been tracking, but we're essentially getting paid to carry insurance.

Our health insurance costs us $3,000 each year, but these payments are deducted from my wife's paycheck before paying any taxes, saving us $1,132. Then, by maxing out our HSA we're saving another $1,812 in taxes. And, finally, my wife's employer pays us $2,400, just because we purchased an HDHP.

In essence, that means that we'll be about $2,344 richer at the end of the year, because we signed up for the right medical insurance and knew how to take advantage of the incentives that our plan provided.

Now, I do need to issue a caveat here. Just because a plan has a very high deductible doesn't mean it's actually an HDHP. It must also make you eligible to open an HSA.

Also, not all HDHPs are created equal. Some HDHPs have higher premiums than others. Some employers don't offer employer contributions, and HSAs won't save as much money for somebody in a 12% income tax bracket, living in a place with no state income tax, as they will for somebody in a 32% tax bracket, living in California or New York.

So, how effective this strategy is will depend a lot on your specific circumstances and what types of plans your employer offers.

That said, this is a strategy you should look into closely. Even if it doesn't put money in your pocket, it could easily offset the entire cost of your premiums.

And that brings me to my next point.

Tip #5: An HDHP with an HSA is Almost Always the Most Affordable Type of Plan, Even When You Have a Lot of Medical Bills

"Not so fast," you may interject. "Making money off health insurance is amazing, but that's assuming zero medical costs that year. That won't be us; we're having a baby!"

That's a fair critique. After all, the primary thing that scares people away from HDHPs isn't the cost; it's the risk that they'll need medical care and have to pay that high deductible out-of-pocket. That's reasonable... especially when you <u>know</u> you'll have medical expenses.

But here's the good news.

Even during those years when you know you'll be maxing out your deductible—or even your OOP limit, for that matter—going with an HDHP that has an HSA will almost always save you more money than the other plans offered by the same employer or insurance exchange.

This tends to be true whether your employer contributes to your HSA or not. And, of course, I'm assuming that you actually max out your HSA for the tax benefits.

Let me give you an example.

You remember that Cadillac plan with a really low $1,000 family deductible that my wife's employer offers? If we were on that plan and had a car crash that put our entire family in the ICU with a million dollars of medical expenses, causing us to max out our OOP limits, we would be $10,869 poorer at the end of the year.

Now, let's assume we had the same catastrophe on our current HDHP with an HSA. That plan would only leave us $3,656 poorer at the end of the year! Remember, that's after accounting for every possible cost and incentive associated with holding this insurance plan—premiums, coinsurance, deductibles, tax savings, etc.

So, by going with that "scary" HDHP that has a deductible four times larger than the expensive Cadillac insurance plan, my family would end up paying about a third as much money, under a worst-case medical emergency.

Not only is this true for the plans my wife's employer offers, it was also true of my last two employers. It even holds true on government-run insurance exchanges.

For example, those government HDHP plans don't offer you any sort of employer contributions to your HSA, and some charge premiums that are actually <u>higher</u> than non-HSA-eligible plans. Yet, in the end, HDHP plans with an HSA still win out in a worst-case medical scenario over non-HDHP plans without an HSA.

The two HSA-eligible plans that were available on the government-run insurance exchange in my zip code beat out every single other plan available on that exchange.

Now, there are a few caveats to be mindful of here, too. In most cases, an HDHP with an HSA will be the best option available to you, but there are always exceptions. So, you need to know how to spot a bad HDHP, and here are a few things to look for.

A really good HDHP will have premiums that are at least as low (and hopefully much lower) than other plans your employer offers from the same provider. If your employer is willing to contribute to your HSA on your behalf, that's especially promising.

Also, you want to look at your plan's OOP limits. Make sure they're on par with the other plans that your employer offers. If they are significantly higher than those other plans, you may need to run the numbers to find out which plan really is the best in your situation.

Where this gets difficult is when you need to compare plans across providers to find out which one is best. So, remember that you can't simply assume that an HDHP from a crappy provider will automatically be better than non-HDHP plans from a different provider. You have to run the numbers.

For example, in almost every case, any insurance plan from a government-run exchange, even an HDHP, is going to cost you more than the worst plan your employer offers, whether it's an HDHP or not.

And, what about the sticker shock of having to potentially pay that high deductible all at once? Well, by funneling the money you're saving on premiums into maxing out your HSA, you'll be prepared to pay for the medical bills, even if they come all at once.

Tip #6: Some HMO Plans Can be Even More Affordable than HDHPs When Having a Baby, but HMOs Come with Constraints

In my quest for the most affordable health insurance, I need to mention Health Management Organizations (HMOs). Depending on how they're structured, HMOs can sometimes beat out HDHPs as the most cost-effective option if you know you'll be having a baby. But, they aren't without their drawbacks.

HMOs tend to only provide service to a limited geographic area. They contract with doctors in that area to be part of their network, or they hire doctors to work directly for them. Part of how they keep costs low is to refuse coverage for out-of-network care, unless it's an emergency.

That may not be a problem if your HMO has a good selection of doctors or specialists in their network. The thing is, a lot of times, you won't know whether they do until you go to find your doctor. So, it wouldn't be surprising if your partner was stuck seeing a doctor she doesn't trust. This is probably the biggest drawback of HMOs.

Another drawback is the fact that they tend to require referrals from your primary-care doctor if you need any sort of specialist services. And, in the same vein, they might require you to get certain services "pre-approved" or they could refuse coverage.

With all that said, HMOs can make a lot of sense if your partner finds a doctor she likes who's in the HMO's network, and if the facility where she plans to give birth is also covered.

If you're thinking of going this route when your baby comes, there are a few more important caveats to know about.

Not all HMOs are created equal. To find the ones that are worth having, you need to look for these three characteristics: 1) no deductibles, 2) reasonable copays without any coinsurance obligations, and 3) reasonable premiums.

Most non-HMO insurance plans have a sizeable deductible and coinsurance (e.g. 30%) that you have to pay on the remainder of your bill, even after you've met your deductible.

I've seen plenty of HMO plans structured like this, too —mostly on government-run exchanges. And there's nothing about them that makes them more affordable than non-HMO plans. They function just like most other plans, but with more restrictions on which doctors you can see. These are not the droids you're looking for.

There are, however, some HMO insurance plans that are structured completely differently. These tend to have either no deductible at all or a very, very modest one. And, instead of making you pay coinsurance, they charge a pre-determined, flat-rate copay for the services you and your family need.

On plans like these, the copays for childbirth and delivery might only be a few hundred dollars. You can find out how much they are by looking at the plan's Summary of Benefits and Coverage (SBC) document before you ever sign up for the plan.

Also, just like with every other type of plan, if the premiums on your HMO are a lot higher than the other plans you have to choose from, the HMO probably won't be your best option.

For example, one of the insurance plans that my wife's company offers for employees in California is an HMO with monthly premiums of almost $800. That plan even has a $0 deductible and low copay for childbirth, yet it was among the worst-performing employer-sponsored plans I analyzed because the premiums are so high.

On the flip side, let me illustrate how an HMO that's structured the right way can save you so much money.

Another, much better, HMO plan that my wife's company offers has more reasonable premiums ($236 per month), as well as a $0 deductible. It also doesn't charge anything for prenatal office visits, and the copays for giving birth at the hospital and "admitting" the baby after birth are $350 each.

So, if you purchased this plan, your out-of-pocket expense for a $29,000 pregnancy and childbirth would be roughly $700. After premiums, you'd only be $2,766 poorer at the end of the year. Not bad for a year when you had a baby!

That's compared to $8,381 poorer at the end of the year if you had instead opted for that Cadillac health insurance plan with the low family deductible, which I mentioned earlier. And compared to $3,460 poorer by going with the HDHP we chose.

If we'd chosen that HMO instead of the HDHP, we'd have saved $694 but not been able to go with the healthcare provider my wife preferred.

So, not all HMO insurance plans are worth buying, but if they're structured the right way and your partner is comfortable with the in-network health care providers that she has to choose from, they can be the most affordable insurance option available to you during years when you know or suspect that you'll have large medical expenses.

Tip #7: You're Not Stuck with Whatever Insurance Plan You Currently Have

If, after reading this far, you realize that you made a terrible mistake the last time you chose your health insurance, don't worry. There's still a way out.

You're not stuck with the plan you've already got just because your baby is due before the next open enrollment period—the time of year (usually in the fall) when everybody is allowed to switch insurance plans.

It's true; normally, people aren't allowed to change their health insurance plans, except during open enrollment.

But, there are exceptions for major life changes, called "qualifying life events". These include things like losing your current insurance coverage (e.g. changing jobs), moving to a different zip code or county, and having a baby.

After your baby is born, you'll have 30-60 days to either add your baby to your current policy or switch health insurance plans completely. The new policy will cover your baby retroactively to his birth date and normally cover mom's delivery costs, too.

If you've chosen a really bad insurance policy and you know it, this is a tremendous opportunity to take advantage of the strategies I've taught you above, because you can switch insurance and have it retroactively cover childbirth, which accounts for the vast majority of medical costs associated with pregnancy.

When our first daughter was born, less than 13% of that $29,000 was spent before the delivery. But, over $25,000 of the total cost was billed to the new insurance plan that we chose.

But, before changing insurance plans, there are two really important considerations you need to take into account.

Every time you change insurance plans, all of your deductibles and OOP limits reset. So, if your baby isn't due until your new plan year starts after the next open enrollment period, you can choose the best plan available at that time, when your deductibles will reset anyway.

If you switch plans in the middle of the year (instead of during open enrollment), you could end up needlessly paying two deductibles. It can still make sense to do so, but you have to be careful. It may make sense if you haven't had a lot of expenses before you switch, but it will never make sense if you've already come close to meeting your family OOP limit for the year.

Secondly, you need to consider how much you've already paid in premiums on your current plan, as well as how much more you still have to pay for the year.

If you're currently on a really low-deductible plan and you've had the plan for nine months when your baby comes, it probably doesn't make sense to switch because premiums are where you would save money on a different plan, but you'll have already paid most of them for the year. Instead, take advantage of those low deductibles that you've been paying for, and avoid causing them to reset by switching.

By contrast, if you've already chosen an expensive insurance policy but you'll still be in the first half of your plan year when your baby arrives, it may make sense to switch to a more affordable plan, since you'll have more time during the year to take advantage of the new plan's lower premiums and HSA tax savings, if applicable.

Whether it does or doesn't make sense to switch health insurance plans mid-year always requires a bit of analysis because it depends on when your baby will be born, in relation to the end of your plan year, as well as what plan you're currently on and what your other options are.

Tip #8: You May Be Able to Cut Pregnancy-Related Medical Costs by as Much as 80% without Any Insurance

So far, all of these strategies have revolved around choosing the best insurance policy. So, what if you just don't have good insurance options to choose from?

If you're self-employed or the company you work for doesn't offer any reasonably-priced policies, don't let that keep you up at night.

You're not doomed to purchase an overpriced Obamacare policy from a government exchange and still spend tens of thousands of dollars for your child's birth.

I've already mentioned that the total medical cost from conception to delivery for our fourth baby was about $6,000, and it would have been about $5,000 if we hadn't switched medical providers mid-pregnancy. And that was the total cost billed, not just what we paid out-of-pocket.

So, how did we go from $29,000 with our third child to $5,000 with our fourth child? Hint: it had nothing at all to do with insurance.

My wife delivered our first kid at a hospital with an OBGYN, and neither of us had a good experience with any of the doctors involved. We knew there had to be a better way.

So, for our second and third children, we decided to go with a midwife, who had rights to deliver in the hospital. And that certainly helped because the midwife was more open to my wife's preferences. For example, when labor stalled with our second son, she didn't jump straight to inducing labor with Pitocin, and my wife was not forced to deliver our kids while laying flat on her back in a hospital bed—apparently one of the most unnatural positions for childbirth.

For what we wanted, a midwife-assisted delivery at a hospital seemed perfect, until we moved to a new area where we were not at all impressed with the hospitals.

Yet, we kept hearing friends (and even strangers) recommend a local birthing center. So we decided to give it a try. This single decision cut our medical bill by about 80%.

How is that possible?!

With our fourth kid, we paid $4,050 for the midwife's services, which included use of the birthing center, help with delivery, prenatal checkups, and a post-partum visit at our house.

Compare that to just the hospital bill with our third child, which was a whopping $18,916 by itself. That didn't include doctor's fees, prenatal lab work, pediatrician services, or anything else... mostly just use of the hospital.

Oh, and the birthing center provided all required lab testing at cost for the entire pregnancy. So, lab tests for which we might've been billed $150 each at a hospital or OBGYN's office cost us less than $5 each through the birthing center. That's really saying something when you consider that over 10% ($3,147) of the cost associated with our third child's birth was for lab work alone.

Understand, too, that this is about far more than just saving money. My wife says that having our daughter with a midwife at a birthing center was BY FAR her best birthing experience. We both wish we had known this with our other kids.

If your partner is willing to consider a natural birth (i.e. no epidural), going with a birthing center and a midwife is definitely a strategy you should consider.

This isn't some inferior option just for people who don't have insurance. It can be used in tandem with insurance, and often makes sense to do so. While some insurance plans won't cover birthing centers, others will.

What's more, even if your insurance plan won't cover an out-of-hospital birth, it still may make sense to go this route. That's what happened with us.

Our insurance didn't cover a penny of our fourth child's birth because our birthing center wasn't in-network. But that didn't matter. The total cost of the services they provided was just a hair over our policy's deductible anyway, and they provided a standard of care that was far superior to what we could have gotten at our local hospitals.

The icing on the cake is that, even though our insurance plan didn't cover any of our costs, we were still able to benefit from a lot of the other strategies that I've already covered. We still paid the lowest premiums of any plan available to us and had coverage in case we did have a real medical emergency at some point. We continued receiving an employer contribution to our HSA, and we still reduced our tax burden by maxing out our HSA.

When you take all of that into account, we only ended up paying about $300 more out-of-pocket for our fourth child's birth than it would've cost us to go to an in-network provider at a hospital; yet, we received better care.

Now, just imagine if your only insurance option was one of those plans I mentioned earlier from the government exchange. Even if you qualified for the massive subsidies mentioned, they would have almost certainly required your partner to give birth at a hospital with an OBGYN.

And, yeah, you would've had insurance coverage. But, if you assume the total bill came in at $29,000, it would've cost your family somewhere <u>between $8,000 and $21,000 more</u> than delivering at a birthing center without any insurance coverage, depending on the plan you chose.

Stop Following the Herd

Each of these strategies is tried and true, with real numbers and experiences to back it up, but they certainly aren't mainstream strategies.

I've heard people caution others, "You've got to be careful with plans that have high deductibles," without ever considering the bigger picture of all the costs and potential savings.

Or a typical reaction when people find out my wife delivered at a birthing center, "Wow, you're brave.

What if something had gone wrong?" They automatically dismiss the option, without realizing that many birthing centers are right next to hospitals for that very reason.

Is mainstream what you want to go with? Between the birthing horror stories my wife hears regularly and the heavy financial burden people normally assume when having a child the conventional way, I think I'll pass.

I know it's not comfortable trusting your own judgment when everybody around you is screaming that you're crazy... but neither is shelling out the equivalent of a down payment on a house when you have a kid.

Now at least you can make an informed choice, equipped with strategies and the reasons behind them, to better cover your medical bills, potentially improve your insurance options, and not sacrifice your family's quality of care.

15

DAILY EXPENSES – WHAT IT ACTUALLY COSTS TO RAISE A KID

A lot of first-time dads are apprehensive about what it actually costs to raise a kid, even after you get past the medical expenses of having one in the first place.

That's completely understandable, since most of what you'll read about having kids makes it seem like you're signing up for indentured servitude and impending financial apocalypse.

But, don't worry. Most of what you've read is wrong.

One of the most pervasive sources cited by articles and blogs on this topic is a study published every few years by the US Department of Agriculture (USDA). This study is as close to an "official number" as you're going to get in the US when it comes to the cost of raising a kid from birth through 17 years old. And, sadly, its alarming findings are regurgitated all over the internet, by people who likely don't even have kids and don't know what they're talking about.

According to the USDA, raising one kid from birth through 17 years old costs parents in the ballpark of $284,570—and that's just for necessities like food and shelter. It doesn't touch childbirth or college education.[1]

If you're as gobsmacked as I was at that number, hang onto your seat. We're going to blow our learned friends and their research out of the water. But first, let's unpack how they arrived at this staggering figure.

- Housing is the No. 1 cost-driver, at 29% of the total budget
- Then comes food, 18% of the total cost per child (food costs spike from $300 to $900 per year for teenagers)
- Childcare and education (not including college) makes up 16%
- Transportation makes up 15% (the study considers driving age, insurance, and buying a second car)
- Basic healthcare (not including childbirth) totals 9%

- Clothing makes up 6%
- All other costs associated with child-rearing come up to 7%

Don't Worry, The USDA is Lying

We've got four kids, so I have a really good idea of what they cost, day-to-day. I was in a state of shock when I read these figures. Our kids aren't out of the house yet, but we've had them long enough to know that something is massively wrong with the USDA's study. So, take heart.

With some more digging, I found a separate study published by William Comanor, an economist from UC Berkley's School of Health Policy and Management.[2] He uses the exact same data as the USDA but comes up with much more realistic results.

Comanor found that the total cost of raising a first child, for someone in the low or middle-income group, is less than one-third of the USDA's estimate! And even for high-income households, the cost was less than half the USDA's number.

So, what gives?! Why the difference?!

First off, the USDA's number is ridiculously inflated because it includes tons of expenses that are either optional or that couples would have whether they were parents or not. By contrast, Comanor <u>only</u> included costs incurred for child-rearing that would not have been incurred without kids.

Next, the USDA takes a one-size-fits-all approach by averaging the spending of families across different income categories. But here's the thing; some parents spend far more on their kids than other parents. What's more, how much most people spend on their kids is determined more by what they make than what their kids actually need.

So, taking an average of those numbers to figure out what it costs to raise a kid is as crazy as averaging Paris Hilton's annual expenses with your neighbor's and saying, *"That's what it costs to live in America!"*

The reason Comanor's numbers are much more realistic is that he took a more methodical approach, comparing the costs of child-rearing based on each household's income bracket (low, middle, and high) and the number of kids (one, two, or three-plus children).

So, using Comanor's findings, we can safely cut that number from the USDA by 67%, from about $285,000 to about $94,000 for an "average" family. That only comes out to an average of a little over $5,000 per year, to raise your first kid.

And, if you're hoping to have more kids, the good news is that they get cheaper as you go. Comanor found that second kids are always cheaper than first kids, and the total cost of raising three or more children is no greater than the cost of raising two kids, for low and middle-income households.

Now, I think Comanor gives us a much more realistic idea of how much it costs to raise a kid, but I'm not convinced he was totally on the money either.

Here's why. When we had our first child, we were living in Vienna, VA—a suburb of Washington, DC with a very high cost of living—renting a one-bedroom basement apartment. In our son's first year, we only spent an average of $100 more per month ($1,200 for the year) on all expenses combined: diapers, groceries, nursing pads, baby wipes, baby vitamins, baby bottles, formula, etc. This number includes everything except medical and childcare.

Yes, I'm sure that number is lower than it would've been if we hadn't received baby shower gifts, but that doesn't explain such a massive difference by itself.

What we spent on day-to-day necessities was only about 8% of the annual cost that the USDA estimated for a middle-income family with their first child, and only 25% of Comanor's estimate. And, even then, we were living in a very high-cost-of-living area, but our son was happy, healthy, and lacked absolutely nothing.

This wasn't a fluke either. The next year, we had our second child and had to move because we needed more space. Even with the increased rent, our monthly expenses for that second year were pretty much right on Comanor's estimate for a middle-income family with two kids, but our spending was still only 29% of what the USDA projected.

The bottom line is that you can't trust the "official numbers" that everybody bandies around and uses to scare new parents to death. They're massively inflated and don't reflect reality for most people.

Raising a Kid Without Going Broke: Practical Tips

Now that I've put to rest any Google-induced panic about the alleged financial ruin that inevitably awaits you and every other new dad, let me break down what you *should* expect for some of these key baby-related costs as well as teach you how to keep them under control without sacrificing your standard of living.

I've split the costs you'll face for the first few years into five main categories: baby formula, baby food, disposable diapers, clothing, and baby gear.

. . .

Tip #1: Baby Formula – "Breast is Best"

Parents who 100% bottle-feed their babies can expect to spend between $1,200 and $1,500 on baby formula during their baby's first year.[3] Breastfeeding, on the other hand, is basically free, and most insurance plans will even pay for a breast pump. Breastfeeding is also much healthier for your kid. There's really no comparison. In fact, breast milk is in such high demand among moms who can't breastfeed that there are online marketplaces where moms with excess milk can sell it for $1 - $2.5 per ounce.

There's just one important caveat here, though. Breast-feeding can be unpredictable. Some new mothers find that they're physically unable to breastfeed. Others, especially working women, may choose not to for personal reasons, so you and your partner should discuss the pros and cons and figure out what's most important for your family.

Tip #2: Baby Food – You Don't Need Gerbers

Normally, when your kid is around six months old, you'll be able to start introducing baby food. Buying organic baby food from the store will cost between $155 and $210 per month (or about $45 - $115 for non-organic), but there's no need to spend that much money.[4] A major way we saved with our first child was making our own organic baby food. You can do this for only about $30 per month.[5]

We saved somewhere between $1,500 and $2,500 during the first year, just by throwing some veggies we were already preparing in a food processor! This isn't a heavy lift; you can even make it ahead of time and freeze it in an ice cube tray for baby-sized servings ready to be thawed when needed. And as your baby grows older, you can simply puree and feed him whatever you're already cooking for yourselves. That way he won't be too picky when it's time to introduce solid foods.

Tip #3: Diapers – Opt for Store-Brand, Buy in Bulk, Potty Train Early

Disposable diapers could cost you up to $2,445 during the first three years of your baby's life, if you're not smart about how you purchase.[6] My biggest recommendation here is to buy in bulk. Well-known name-brand disposables, if bought in bulk (between 128 and 144 per box), can cost as little as $0.22 each, as opposed to $0.60 per diaper. Even expensive name-brand, eco disposable diapers can cost below $0.30 each when bought in bulk, for those babies who are sensitive to regular diapers.

Secondly, try out some of the store-brand disposables, instead of the go-to name brands. Brand name diapers —even if bought in bulk—just aren't worth the cost. Because every baby's bottom is shaped differently, each brand of diapers performs differently from one kid to another. For each of our kids, we found a store brand that worked as well as or better than the name brand varieties. We're currently buying diapers for $0.09 each.

Another thing you may want to consider is potty-training 'early'. Doing so could not only save you thousands of dollars, but it's also more hygienic for your kid and can save you a ton of hassle. Changing any diaper is unpleasant, but changing a diaper on a three-year-old is especially so.

We waited until about 25 months to potty train our oldest. That's earlier than average for a boy in the US, but even at that age, potty training can become a power struggle. We potty trained our second at 19 months, with much less of a struggle than with our first, and we potty trained our third at 15 months with similar ease.

While these are much earlier ages than average in the US, they're actually quite late compared to many parts of the world where people can't afford diapers.

. . .

Tip #4: Clothing – You're Not Too Good for Goodwill

Buying clothing is another area to watch out for. The USDA says that 6% of annual costs in their figure go to purchasing clothes. That means that an average income couple would spend $625 per year, just on clothes for their kid. If the USDA is to be trusted, from the time our oldest son was born until now we would have spent $7,500, just to buy clothes for our kids! Not even close.

Don't get me wrong; it is *possible* to spend $625 per year on baby clothes, but it's also insane and completely unnecessary.

When we had our first kid, we were blessed to have some friends a few years ahead of us in starting their families, and they generously shared various baby items that we needed. When you have a baby, you'll probably find that a lot of coworkers, friends, and neighbors start giving you baby items, too. In fact, they may give you more stuff than you can even use.

Of course, we still had to buy plenty of clothes. Especially when our first daughter came along and we couldn't re-use the clothes we had. But our approach was practical, so we bought a big box of girls' 0-6 month baby clothes for $20 from a family selling them on Craigslist.

Remember, babies could care less whether they're spitting up or pooping in a designer-label onesie... parents are the ones who care about that. If you're intent on having that particular logo on your baby's clothes, ask yourself whether you're just trying to satisfy your own status insecurities.

You can find lots of brand-new outfits (even with the tags still on them) at Goodwill or other second-hand stores, for only $0.50 or $1 apiece. This is a great way to dress your kid well for just pennies on the dollar.

We now have four children, aged five and younger. Yet, from the birth of our oldest until the publication of this book, I'm certain that our spending on clothing (new and "pre-loved") for all our kids hadn't exceeded $625 total—the USDA's estimate for one_kid's clothes for a single year. And our kids are not poorly dressed in the least, so there you go.

Tip #5: Baby Gear – Less is More

The last big category to talk about is baby gear. I mean everything from changing tables and cribs to car seats and toys. This is definitely a case of 'you don't really know what you need until you really need it', so don't go buying every designer item in matching shades of dove grey or duck egg blue before your baby arrives.

You may be suffering from a common parenting syndrome called "keeping up with the Karda…. ah, the Joneses!"

While some items are necessary, like a car seat or a crib, most of what people buy will only be useful for a short period. Babies grow faster than you can say "wallet". And, before you know it, most of these chic items will be gathering dust in your attic—like that $300 electric baby swing rocker thing that you were only able to use twice, because your baby hated it.

Also, remember that babies need very little to thrive. This includes toys. In fact, having too many is harmful. Researchers have found that having too many toys reduces the quality of a toddler's play. Not only does it reduce their ability to focus and play creatively, it also causes them to *play less* and *share less*. As it turns out, having too much "stuff" is overwhelming for anybody, but especially kids.[7]

Childhood development experts hesitate to put a specific number on how many toys would be healthy for kids to have, but many believe that about two dozen is enough for kids who are preschool age.[8] Bottom line: kids don't need much and what they do need isn't stuff… it's your presence and love.

If you're strapped for cash, don't just go to the store and drop a few thousand dollars on toys, furniture, and clothes. Almost everything you'll need, from toys and books to furniture and clothing, can be borrowed from family or friends or bought "pre-loved" at second-hand stores or on Facebook, eBay, and Craigslist.

The baby industry is a lot like the wedding industry. Marketers prey on customers' emotions, like feelings of guilt and inadequacy or experiences of poverty during childhood. This is purely to get people to pay obscene amounts of money for things that they don't need, and probably don't even want.

By the time our second child arrived, I was convinced that kids need so much less than society prescribes. Don't get me wrong; it's okay to buy nice things for your kids from time to time. But you're not failing them when you don't buy them those designer sneakers or a room full of expensive toys. In reality, sheltering them from the rampant consumerism and materialism that our society is drowning in may be one of the best gifts you can give them as a parent.

Our kids learn from us how much importance to attach to "stuff". By raising them to be materialistic, we set them on a course to repeat a cycle of unhappiness and poor money management into adulthood. We also rob them of the chance to flex the resilience that 'making do' inspires.

If you're worried about not being able to give your kids all the things you never had growing up, don't be. That's not what will make you a good dad; doing so could actually end up crippling them.

And, if you're worried about just making ends meet, know that kids aren't as expensive as anybody lets on, and life always finds a way.

16

CHILDCARE – DID YOU SAY $30,000 PER YEAR?

As a new dad, childcare is the one area of cost where I'd say you should believe the hype. It's super expensive.

How expensive? Well, the average, rural, American family, with both parents working outside the home, pays about $175 per week for childcare—that's $9,100 per year. Meanwhile, families in urban areas spend an average of $260 per week—or, $13,520 per year.[1] And, remember, these are averages, so you could spend a lot more or less, depending on where you live.

Let me give you an example. After our oldest was born, my wife and I both returned to work. At the time, we lived in a suburb of Washington DC, which notoriously has the highest childcare costs of any metro area in the country.

Conventional daycare centers would've had us forking out between $1,300 and $2,500 **per month**. That's between $15,600 and $30,000 each year, just for daycare for one kid… after taxes.

And even at that price, the waiting lists were so long we would've had to submit an application right after we found out we were pregnant in order to secure a spot for our son.

As a new dad having never done any of this before, it's hard to know what options are even available when it comes to childcare, much less how they compare. So, I'm going to spend the rest of this chapter getting you up to speed and sharing some creative solutions that might work for your family.

So, What Are Your Options?

About 40% of all kids in the US aged 0-5, who aren't enrolled in kindergarten yet, are cared for by a stay-at-home parent. About 35% go to some sort of center-based care, like a commercial daycare center, preschool, or prekindergarten. Another 25% are cared for by a relative, and about 13% are taken care of in a private home by someone they're not related to—for example, a nanny or an in-home daycare.[2] If you're wondering why these add up to more than 100%, it's because some kids have more than one childcare arrangement in place.

Regardless of which arrangement you end up choosing, there're a few money-saving strategies that anyone in the US who pays for childcare should look into:

1. Setting up a Dependent Care Flexible Spending Account
2. Claiming the Child and Dependent Care Tax Credit
3. Seeing whether your income would allow you to qualify for subsidies from the childcare and development fund

Tax Tips You Need to Know

Dependent Care FSAs: These are special accounts that allow you to set aside money that you don't pay taxes on in order to cover childcare costs up to a certain amount each year. The IRS sets new limits each year to adjust for inflation.

Child and Dependent Care Tax Credit: This is a tax refund to working parents for a percentage of qualifying childcare expenses, up to certain limits. The amount you can claim depends on how many kids you have and what your total household income is. The IRS changes the percentages and limits for this tax credit each year to account for inflation.

I won't delve into the details of these strategies because I'm not a CPA, but I will say that they have the potential of saving you several thousand dollars a year. Look into them.

But, how do you choose a specific childcare arrangement? Which one is best?

Well, this is more than just a math problem. The ultimate goal is to find out what gives your kid the best care and your family the best quality of life, for the lowest price possible. But, unlike health insurance, there aren't solutions that work for pretty much anyone, regardless of circumstances. And each family's circumstances look different.

For example, you and your partner will almost certainly provide better care for your kid than anybody else, but that has to be balanced with other considerations, like your ability to pay the bills and your family's overall quality of life (e.g. career disruption, free time with your kids, the length of your commute, etc.).

Some of this'll come down to factors that are either completely outside of your control or hard to change, like what options are available where you live, how much you make, and what kind of support network you have.

Stay-at-home care is probably not possible if you're a single dad... you still need to make a living. Likewise, it could be that there is no center-based care near you if you live in a very rural area. And, while hiring a nanny might sound wonderful, it just doesn't make financial sense unless both you and your partner's jobs pay a lot more than the nanny's salary.

With all that in mind, there are four childcare arrangements worth considering: center-based care, family daycares, nannies, and stay-at-home care. Having a relative watch your kid is another option, but I'm not going to get into that because it looks so different for every family.

Working Couples' Go-To Choice – Center-Based Care

For kids five and under, center-based care is the most common arrangement for families where both parents work outside the home.

Daycare centers vary a lot. Some of them more-or-less just take care of your kids' needs and let them play while you're at work while others are more formal, with all sorts of programs and enrichment activities.

This structured activity in a social context is appealing to some parents, but having your kid in a group setting for hours on end, five days a week, isn't always a positive thing, especially for infants and toddlers who're younger than three.

Studies have found that children who attend daycare produce much higher levels of the stress-inducing hormone cortisol–known as the "fight-or-flight" hormone—than kids who stay at home.[3] When kids are that young, being away from home in a group setting for the whole day may not be ideal so long as they have a good home life and other options are available.

Another type of daycare center worth looking into are those run by non-profits in your community, like churches and YMCAs. You may find that these daycares operate in a way that's more in-line with your family's personal values, and they could cost considerably less than a commercial daycare center… if there are open spots.

Similar Care, Less Money – Family Daycares

Family daycares, which are often started by somebody who wants to keep earning money but needs to watch their own kids, are also worth considering. While enrollment at family daycares is less than half that of center-based care, they're often a better option.

No, they won't have the same status appeal as the local Montessori preschool, and they probably won't promise as many fancy programs as the local daycare center. But, they also won't come with the same hefty price tag, and they will still have activities, games, and opportunities for your kid to socialize.

One of my brothers lives in a small town near where we grew up, and he only pays $100 per week for his 18-month old daughter to go to a family daycare. By contrast, the cheapest commercial daycare in the area charges $128 per week. A 28% price hike in one of your family's largest annual expenses is a big deal.

Another benefit is that family daycares are often more personal for both kids and parents. Depending on the daycare, your kid may benefit from better child-to-caregiver ratios and less caregiver turnover, plus you'll benefit from dealing directly with the owner, who has more motivation to maintain standards than the average employee might.

Does It Ever Make Sense? – Hiring a Nanny

An even rarer option people choose is hiring a nanny. About the only exposure most people have to nannies is watching The Nanny Diaries or Mary Poppins.

We were shocked to discover that hiring a nanny where we lived actually made financial sense, and it provided a lot of non-financial advantages as well.

First, let's talk about cost, since the stereotype seems to be that nannies are only for the ultra rich who have kids but don't actually want to raise them. The average hourly rate of a nanny is anywhere between $11 and $25 per hour, but it varies according to your area's cost of living.[4]

As I mentioned before, daycare is very expensive where we were living when our first kid was born, so the cost of hiring a nanny was in line with our other options. Also, we knew we wanted more kids, and once a second or third child enters the picture, nannies become more affordable than most daycare centers, even when you factor in those centers' sibling discounts. When our second child came along, our nanny was costing us around 30-40% less than sending both our kids to daycare.

But, even with one kid, once you put a dollar value on the "intangible" benefits of hiring a nanny versus using a daycare, nannies become a lot more affordable.

Here's why: if you already have more work than hours in the day, you can include a few extra responsibilities, such as light cleaning, cooking, and laundry in the job description. This is what we did because our days and evenings were already hectic enough without a baby in the picture. Our nanny not only provided really high-quality care for our son, but she also helped with some other things around the house, which freed us up to spend some time in the evenings with our kid.

Also, unlike a daycare, hiring a nanny means your kid isn't going to be crowded out by 15 other kids in class. And, you have final say in how your kid is raised while you're at work. This is huge.

This option also doesn't require a longer commute or bending your workday around daycare drop-offs and pickups. Oh, and when your kid gets sick, your nanny will still show up, so you don't have to unexpectedly take time off work.

Here's the thing, though; if you live in an area with low childcare costs or you only have one kid that needs to be cared for, hiring a nanny is only going to make sense if you and your partner both have salaries making a good bit more than what you would have to pay the nanny.

If the going rate of nannies in your area falls outside of your budget, yet you badly want to avoid a daycare center, think of offering a more creative compensation structure. It can take the form of a weekly salary, health benefits, paid vacation, etc–perks that most people don't offer for nanny jobs.

Another viable option is to form a *nanny share,* meaning the nanny cares for two or more families' kids as a group, while still providing a lot more individualized care for each child than they would get at a daycare center.

Hidden Benefits & Practical Tips – Staying Home

Increasingly, it's such a given that mom and dad will both go back to work after parental leave, that one of you staying home to take care of your kid doesn't even come up for discussion. If your household is dual income, it probably seems logical that anything less than that will spell instant bankruptcy. But, you may not realize how much money you can save by one partner staying home, or the huge quality of life improvement that decision can have for the entire family.

We very seriously considered one of us quitting our job when our first kid was born, especially after looking at the cost of childcare. This option isn't for everybody, though. Some people would go crazy without having the social and mental outlet that their jobs provide, no matter how much they love their kids. Some people just can't make ends meet without the extra income, and others would jettison their careers by taking off several years from work.

However, having one parent stay home has a lot of other benefits.

As with a nanny, it eliminates the daily pick-up and drop-off routine, which can easily add as much as two hours to your commute in urban areas. You also don't have to worry about paying hefty fees every time you pick your kid up late because you got held up in traffic. Nor do you have the hassle of somebody needing to take vacation every day that your kid has so much as a runny nose.

All of these have value. It's just hard to compare it with what you're giving up by quitting your job.

Now, I'm not saying being a stay-at-home parent is all lollipops and sunshine. It's not easy, and it has a huge financial cost of its own... your job. But losing that second income doesn't need to be as scary as it is for most people. Here are some considerations to put things into perspective.

Tip #1: Look at the Long-Term Impact

In our case, one of the reasons we decided it'd be best for us both to return to work, even though we would've preferred for one of us to stay home, was that we were both in highly specialized fields.

If either of us had left the workforce for several years, it would've been very hard to re-enter our fields later. Even if we were able to, we would've taken a serious pay cut and demotion. And that's on top of several years' worth of lost pay increases, promotions, and retirement benefits.

Having said that, I need to give a caveat. I've talked a lot about money in these past few chapters, but that's because I'm addressing new dads' most common fears about making ends meet. So long as you're paying the bills, money absolutely shouldn't be the final decision maker in any of this. It's just important to make each decision with a clear understanding of its costs and benefits.

Not every parent is in the situation we were in. Perhaps your job is in a field that's not highly specialized, in which case you can probably re-enter the workforce with relative ease.

Or, perhaps one of you hates your job and is ready for a career change. So, if you can afford tuition costs along with added baby expenses, why not use the 4-5 years that you'll be out of the workforce, to learn the skills and get the credentials you'll need to change careers. That employment gap will be irrelevant if you're going to start from scratch in your new field anyway. Talk about lemonade from lemons!

Tip #2: Having a Job Costs Money, Too

For example, have you figured out how many times a month you've bought take-out because you were both too tired to cook after a hard day at work? Add the cost of commuting, parking fees, car insurance, "dressing for success", grabbing morning coffee and lunch at your favorite café, and you're looking at hundreds, if not thousands, of (after-tax) dollars in expenses that would fall away with one partner at home.

Tip #3: Staying Home Can Save You Money in Other Areas

With one of you at home, there are tons of opportunities to save money and improve your entire family's quality of life in other ways.

If one of you is home, you'll have the flexibility to do the grocery shopping, pack lunches, and cook dinner. You can shop around for bargains and better products, instead of whatever you grab in those last-minute store runs that you do on the way home from work. Not only would you save on your grocery bill, but your family can eat healthier at home, work, and school!

You can also take the chaotic after-work rush out of the equation. Fewer chores in the evenings mean more family time and maybe even some time for hobbies.

Tip #4: Nobody Said You Can't Earn Money as a Stay-at-Home Parent

Why not use the high cost of childcare to your advantage by starting your own family daycare? I mean, one of you will be home watching your kid anyway.

Alternatively, if you want to keep your skills in your given field sharp, consider working as a digital freelance consultant. You get to do what you're already good at, in your own space, and adapt it to suit your schedule. Yeah, you'll find yourself doing work after the baby is down for bed, or when your partner get's home from work, but you may never want to return to an office again!

While starting your own business may not be something you or your partner have ever considered before, don't disregard this. It can make a huge difference for your family. I know it did for mine when I was a kid.

Soon after having kids, my mom tried going back to work to help pay the bills, and had to rely on a family daycare. Then one day, she'd had enough of the struggle to make ends meet while feeling like she was missing out. The balance between family time and money was off.

She started crunching some numbers and made a shocking discovery. She was paying the bulk of her take-home earnings so a stranger could take care of her kids. All she got was a few scraps of quality time at the end of the day.

That's when my mom made probably the most important decision of our childhood. She gave up her job to care for us, and then, because she knew we'd be stretched on just one income, she started a small home-based business raising and selling puppies.

To everyone's surprise, the puppy business quickly grew to cover about half of my parents' total income. Life was beautiful and simple. My mom was still able to earn money without paying for childcare and got to spend a lot more time with us.

And, yeah, I'm talking about my mom in this example, but in an era of flexible schedules, remote work, and teleconferencing, this can make just as much sense for a dad.

Childcare is no picnic, and it's certainly going to place its own demands on you, but with an honest look at your family's needs and values as well as a good dose of boldness and creativity, you can come out of it even better than you went in, with some well-loved and cared-for kids in tow.

LEAVE A 1-CLICK REVIEW

I would be incredibly thankful if you would take just 30 seconds to leave a review with your honest feedback on Amazon. Your review is essential to help other dads find this book and know it will prepare them for fatherhood. It'll only take 30 seconds... just two or three sentences about what you found most valuable, your favorite chapters, etc!

Visit this link!
https://www.amazon.com/review/create-review/?asin=B0B197N3JJ
Or scan the QR code below!

CONCLUSION

It was early afternoon, about a week before Christmas, and my wife had taken time off work so she could pick me up from the airport. I'd just gotten back from a business trip overseas and was excited to catch up on everything that'd happened during the month I was away.

As we rolled into the driveway, my wife casually mentioned, "I'm so glad it worked out for us to come and pick you up." For a moment, I was confused because our son was at home with our nanny. As I glanced over to see whether I had heard her correctly, a smile came over her face.

"Wait, you're pregnant?" I asked.

"I am. I'm six weeks along!"

It'd been a year and a half since our camping trip in Red Wood National Forest and my surprisingly lackluster response to hearing that my wife was pregnant with our first son. But, oh, what a difference that year and a half had made.

This time, I didn't need any time to process the news... I was over the moon with excitement!

Fatherhood was no longer just some future priority. It wasn't a black box that I knew would change my life for good but didn't fully understand how. I was no longer just trusting that the blessings of fatherhood would outweigh the more visible inconveniences and demands of having kids.

No, fatherhood was real to me. Yeah, it was difficult (and it still is), but it was absolutely amazing.

It was hearing "up dada" first thing in the morning, as my son waited with excitement for the day to begin. It was a hug and a kiss on the way out the door in the morning and a celebration when I got home from work. It was a little head napping on my chest in the afternoon, and a little fist wrapped around my finger. It was stacking blocks together on the living room floor, teaching him how to clap his hands, and cheering at every new thing he learned. It was giving "horsey-back" rides to bed and singing him a lullaby as he drifted off to sleep.

It was the realization that everything in life had more significance with my son watching to learn what it means to be a man. It was coming face-to-face with my own immaturity, selfishness, and shortcomings through the eyes of my son. And it was being overcome by his unconditional love and acceptance in response. It was the inspiration to be the best I could be so that he would have the example he needs and always know he's loved.

Fatherhood was the best thing that had ever happened to me, and I couldn't wait to meet this second little baby, who had already become a part of our family— even though it would be almost another eight months until I got to hold him.

Now, we have four kids: two boys and two girls. I don't just love them… I adore them. And being their dad is the most important thing I will ever do. So, I intend to do it well.

A Final Word

We all have a different starting point.

Perhaps you're like me. You knew you wanted to be a dad long before now and were even *trying* to have kids, but were taken off guard when the time actually came because of concerns you hadn't really worked through.

Or, perhaps you find yourself faced with an unplanned pregnancy. Maybe you were convinced that you're not cut out for fatherhood at all or you just didn't understand why anybody would want all the extra inconvenience and responsibility that kids bring with them.

However you initially responded to the news that you're going to be a dad—exuberant or distraught, overjoyed or terrified, confident or hesitant—I hope the perspective, experiences, and tips that I've shared with you have helped to plant your feet on solid ground.

If there's one thing I want you to take from this book, it's that there's now nothing in your life more important than being the best dad you can be, and it's a role that only you can fill. You're both capable and essential. Your family needs you, so it's time to man up.

When you feel like you won't be able to make ends meet, remember that life always finds a way. I've armed you with some powerful strategies. Now, all you need to do is act on them.

When you feel incompetent as a partner, a caregiver, or a father, just commit to being present and learning through your failure. None of us knew what we were doing when we got started, but we're literally built for fatherhood.

When you feel like you can't manage the stress and competing demands of being a husband, a father, and an employee, remember that your partner is there for you, and your employer does not own you. You're strongest when you and your partner work as a team, so commit to being there for each other, to the gates of hell and back. And, when life makes you choose what to prioritize, be intentional about what you sacrifice. You'll regret it if you let life (or your employer) choose for you.

When the chaos of parenting overwhelms you and you're tempted to feel sorry for yourself, remember that the most meaningful things in life come with responsibility and that happiness—while desirable—is not a life-long purpose worth aiming at. It's an honor to have "dad" as part of your identity. And, that's more important than the hobbies you've given up, the parts of your identity that you've left behind, or the temporary inconveniences that fatherhood brings. Sacrificial responsibility is honorable.

When you feel like the wolves are at the door and you're helpless to protect your family from the pain and suffering in this world, resolve not to run from what you fear. Instead, choose to face it head on, and only run when you're chasing something better.

When you feel like you're a failure, remember that you're not doomed to repeat your own father's mistakes. And remember that your kids don't need you to be perfect. They just need you to be the best dad you can be. Take responsibility for yourself, pursue excellence rather than perfection, and apologize quickly... even if it's for the one thousandth time. There is grace for the humble.

A Call to Action

If you were afraid of becoming a dad when you picked up this book, I hope I've given you confidence. If you were anxious, I hope I've given you peace of mind. If you were excited, I hope I've given you even more enthusiasm.

My goal has been to give every new dad a clear way of thinking about and responding to the most common fears that new dads have. If this book has been an encouragement to you, please leave an honest review on Amazon. It'll only take 30 seconds to write a few sentences about what you found most useful, but you'll be helping me get it in the hands of other new dads who need to hear this message.

Click the link or scan the QR code below right now to leave a review!

https://www.amazon.com/review/create-review/?asin=B0B197N3JJ

A GIFT JUST FOR YOU

THE NEW DAD'S CHECKLIST
EVERYTHING YOU NEED TO DO BEFORE (AND
AFTER) YOUR BABY ARRIVES

- A step-by-step guide designed just for dads
- 30 essential steps to take before your baby arrives
- 14 things dads forget to do during & after delivery
- A simple format that helps you track your progress and get prepared

Visit: www.built4thisbook.com **OR** scan the QR code above

WORKS CITED

20 I Love Lucy Fast Facts. (n.d.). Retrieved March 29, 2021, from Lucy Desi Museum: https://lucy-desi.-com/i-love-lucy-history/fast-facts/

Allar, D. (2019, April 15). *Quitting smoking is easier when couples try together*. Retrieved June 10, 2021, from Cardiovascular Business: https://www.cardiovascular-business.com/topics/vascular-endovascular/quitting-smoking-easier-couples-try-together

Barrett, G., Pendry, E., Peacock, J., Victor, C., Thakar, R., & Manyonda, I. (2005). Women's sexual health after childbirth. *Obstetrics & Gynaecology*, *107*(2), 186-195.

Bousman, L. (2007, November). *The Fine Line of Perfectionism: Is It a Strenght or a Weakness in the Workplace.*

Retrieved July 23, 2021, from University of Nebraska at Lincoln: https://digitalcommons.unl.edu/cgi/viewcontent.cgi?article=1003&context=psychdiss

Burns, D. (1980, November). The Perfectionist's Script for Self-defeat. *Psychology Today*, 34-51.

Carlisle, T. (2013, April 17). *Bull Markets Since 1871: Duration and Magnitude.* Retrieved June 12, 2021, from Greenbackd: https://greenbackd.com/2013/04/17/bull-markets-since-1871-duration-and-magnitude/

Ceder, J. (2020, June 22). *Childcare Costs.* Retrieved March 27, 2021, from Very Well Family: https://www.verywellfamily.com/affording-child-care-4157342

Center for Disease Control and Prevention. (2019, February 26). *Pregnancy-Related Deaths.* Retrieved June 8, 2021, from Center for Disease Control and Prevention: https://www.cdc.gov/reproductivehealth/maternalinfanthealth/pregnancy-relatedmortality.htm

Centers for Disease Control and Prevention. (n.d.). *Preventing Birth Defects.* Retrieved June 9, 2021, from Centers for Disease Control and Prevention: https://www.cdc.gov/ncbddd/birthdefects/prevention.html

Clark, D. (1949, October 1). A Man's Crusade for Easy Childbirth. *Esquire*.

Cleveland Clinic. (2020, August 27). *Stillbirth*. Retrieved June 7, 2021, from Cleveland Clinic: https://my.clevelandclinic.org/health/diseases/9685-stillbirth

Comanor, W. S. (2014). *The Economic Cost of Raising Children*. University of California.

Corcoran, L., Steinley, K., & Grady, S. (2019). *Early Childhood Program Participation, Results from the National Household Education Surveys Program of 2016*. US Department of Education.

Corley, H. (2020, September 20). *Cheap Diapers – 5 Ways to Cut Diaper Costs*. Retrieved March 13, 2021, from Very Well Family: https://www.verywellfamily.com/how-to-cut-diaper-costs-293589

Dauch, C., Imwalle, M., Ocasio, B., & Metz, A. E. (2018). The influence of the number of toys in the environment on toddlers' play. *Infant Behavior and Development, 50*, 78-87.

Davey, G. (2019, May 30). *The Anxiety Epidemic - What's Worrying Our University Students?* Retrieved June 12, 2021, from Papers from Sidcup: https://www.papersfromsidcup.com/graham-daveys-blog/the-anxiety-epidemic-whats-worrying-our-university-students

Deanb. (2018, March). *Paternity Leave in the UK*. Retrieved June 2, 2021, from Dad Info: Because Dads Matter!: https://www.dad.info/article/family/work/paternity-leave/paternity-leave-in-the-uk/

DeMonaco, N. (2017, June 15). *Exercises For New Dads*. Retrieved June 5, 2021, from Coury & Buehler Physical Therapy: https://cbphysicaltherapy.com/exercise-for-new-dads/

Dhar, R. (2014, March 14). *Analyzing Babysitter Price & Gender Data*. Retrieved May 9, 2021, from Priceonomics: https://priceonomics.com/the-babysitting-gender-gap/

Djordjevic, N. (2021, May 21). *34 Eye-Opening Anxiety Statistics & Facts to Know in 2021*. Retrieved June 16, 2021, from MedAlertHelp: https://medalerthelp.org/blog/anxiety-statistics/

Edmonds, R. (2021, June 24). *US ranks last among 46 countries in trust in media, Reuters Institute report finds*. Retrieved June 31, 2021, from Poynter: https://www.poynter.org/ethics-trust/2021/us-ranks-last-among-46-countries-in-trust-in-media-reuters-institute-report-finds/

Eldwin. (2015, November 28). *Bio-Domes: a Reflection of Our Future Kings & Queens*. Retrieved June 31, 2021, from Eldwin: https://eldwin.medium.com/trees-domes-and-our-kings-queens-68b62acc678d

Epidemiology of constipation in North America: a systematic review. (2004). *American Journal of Gastroenterology*, 750-759.

Gardner, A. (n.d.). *4 Myths About Miscarriages*. Retrieved June 7, 2021, from Grow by WebMD: https://www.webmd.com/baby/features/4-myths-about-miscarriages#1

Gholipour, B. (2014, June 14). *5 Ways Fatherhood Changes a Man's Brain*. Retrieved May 7, 2021, from LiveScience: https://www.livescience.com/46322-fatherhood-changes-brain.html#:~:text=A%20puff%20of%20oxytocin%20boosts%20dad%2Dbaby%20bond&text=In%20a%20recent%20study%2C%20re searchers,are%20more%20responsive%20in%20return

Gholipour, B. (2014, February 5). *Epidural May Prolong Labor More Than Thought*. Retrieved May 16, 2021, from LiveScience: https://www.livescience.com/43141-epidurals-prolong-labor.html

Ghose, T. (2013, April 16). *Who's Got Better Baby Sense: Mom or Dad?* Retrieved May 5, 2021, from LiveScience: https://www.livescience.com/28753-dads-identify-babies-cries.html

Growing Up by Macklemore & Ryan Lewis. (n.d.). Retrieved July 15, 2021, from Songfacts: https://www.-songfacts.com/facts/macklemore-ryan-lewis/growing-up

Hatfield, H. (n.d.). *What It Costs to Have a Baby.* Retrieved from WebMD: https://www.webmd.com/baby/features/cost-of-having-a-baby#1

How Dads Affect Their Newborn Babies. (n.d.). Retrieved May 30, 2021, from Dad Info: Because Dads Matter!: https://www.dad.info/article/family/kids/babies/how-dads-affect-newborn-babies/

HOWMUCHISIT.ORG. (2018, August 13). *How Much Does Baby Food Cost?* Retrieved March 13, 2021, from HowMuchIsIt.org: https://www.how-muchisit.org/how-much-does-baby-food-cost/

Huerta, D. (2020, June 16). *Breaking The Cycle Of Absent Fathers.* Retrieved July 9, 2021, from Focus on the Family: https://www.focusonthefamily.com/parenting/breaking-the-cycle-of-absent-fathers/

Johnston, W. M., & Davey, G. C. (1997). The psychological impact of negative TV news bulletins: The catastrophizing of personal worries. *British Journal of Psychology,* 85-91.

Kaufman, G., & Petts, R. J. (2020, August 06). Gendered parental leave policies among Fortune 500 companies. *Community, Work & Family.*

Leake, J., & Robbins, T. (n.d.). *Children Play Less the More.* Retrieved March 15, 2021, from Rense.com: https://rense.com/general8/yots.htm

Livingston, G., & Parker, K. (2019, June 12). *8 facts about American dads.* Retrieved May 21, 2021, from Pew Research Center: https://www.pewresearch.org/fact-tank/2019/06/12/fathers-day-facts/

Manson, M. (n.d.). *It's Not All Your Parents' Fault.* Retrieved July 5, 2021, from Mark Manson: Life Advice That Doesn't Suck: https://markmanson.net/parents

Mayo Clinic. (2021, October 16). *Miscarriage.* Retrieved June 6, 2021, from Mayo Clinic: https://www.mayoclinic.org/diseases-conditions/pregnancy-loss-miscarriage/symptoms-causes/syc-20354298

Mayo Clinic. (n.d.). *Pregnancy after miscarriage: What you need to know.* Retrieved June 8, 2021, from Mayo Clinic: https://www.mayoclinic.org/healthy-lifestyle/getting-pregnant/in-depth/pregnancy-after-miscarriage/art-20044134

Mayo Clinic. (2017, October 2017). *Shaken baby syndrome.* Retrieved May 30, 2021, from Mayo Clinic:

https://www.mayoclinic.org/diseases-conditions/shaken-baby-syndrome/symptoms-causes/syc-20366619

Mayo Clinic Staff. (2020, November 12). *Amniocentesis.* Retrieved June 10, 2021, from Mayo Clinic: https://www.mayoclinic.org/tests-procedures/amniocentesis/about/pac-20392914#:~:text=Miscarriage.,before%2015%20weeks%20of%20pregnancy

National Fatherhood Initiative. (n.d.). *The Proof Is In: Father Absence Harms Children.* Retrieved July 1, 2021, from National Fatherhood Initiative: https://www.fatherhood.org/father-absence-statistic

Nordqvist, C. (2011, September 13). *Men's Testosterone Drops Steeply When Baby Arrives.* Retrieved May 21, 2021, from Medical News Today: https://www.medicalnewstoday.com/articles/234266#1

Odent, M. (2008, April 15). *A top obstetrician on why men should NEVER be at the birth of their child.* Retrieved March 31, 2021, from DailyMail.com: https://www.dailymail.co.uk/femail/article-559913/A-obstetrician-men-NEVER-birth-child.html

Oxford University. (2015, May 18). *First time fathers need more support.* Retrieved May 21, 2021, from University of Oxford:

https://www.ox.ac.uk/news/2015-05-18-first-time-fathers-need-more-support-0

Perfectionism Among Young People Significantly Increased Since 1980s, Study Finds. (2018, January 2). Retrieved July 21, 2021, from American Psychological Association: https://www.apa.org/news/press/releases/2018/01/perfectionism-young-people

Pew Research Center. (2007, January 9). *A Portrait of "Generation Next".* Retrieved July 16, 2021, from Pew Research Center: https://www.pewresearch.org/politics/2007/01/09/a-portrait-of-generation-next/

Pew Research Center. (2013, June 14). *The New American Father.* Retrieved June 3, 2021, from Pew Research Center: https://www.pewresearch.org/social-trends/2013/06/14/the-new-american-father/

Potter, N. (2011, November 7). *More Facebook Friends, Fewer Real Ones, Says Cornell Study.* Retrieved June 2, 2021, from ABC News: https://abcnews.go.com/Technology/facebook-friends-fewer-close-friends-cornell-sociologist/story?id=14896994#.T9dGdI56MfM

Pregnancy and Sex Problems. (n.d.). Retrieved May 26, 2021, from What to Expect: https://www.whattoexpect.com/pregnancy/sex-and-relationships/pregnancy-sex-problems/

Roosevelt, T. (1910, November 4). American Ideals in Education Speech.

Rosen, M., & Kelly, D. (2020, February 14). *Why We Need to Talk More About Male Postpartum Depression.* Retrieved May 29, 2021, from Parents: https://www.parents.com/parenting/dads/sad-dads/

Rosengren, W. R., & DeVault, S. (1963). The sociology of time and space in an obstetric hospital. In E. Friedson, *The Hospital in Modern Society* (pp. 284-285). New York: Free Press.

Schmitt, B. (2018, February 13). *MercyMe's Bart Millard thought his father was going to kill him.* Retrieved July 2, 2021, from The Tennessean: https://www.tennessean.com/story/entertainment/music/2018/02/13/bart-millard-mercyme-can-only-imagine-movie-book-father-abuse/320728002/

Schochet, L. (2019, June 04). *5 Facts To Know About Child Care in Rural America.* Retrieved March 23, 2021, from Center for American Progress: https://www.americanprogress.org/issues/early-childhood/news/2019/06/04/470581/5-facts-know-child-care-rural-america/

Shapiro, G. (n.d.). *Seven Fears Expectant Fathers Face.* Retrieved May 01, 2021, from BabyCenter:

https://www.babycenter.com/pregnancy/relation-ships/seven-fears-expectant-fathers-face_8247

Simon, J. (2019, May 07). *The Cost of Baby Formula.* Retrieved March 13, 2021, from SmartAsset: https://smartasset.com/financial-advisor/the-cost-of-baby-formula

Sparrow, D. (2005, October 2). *Fathers Bond With Babies in Different Ways.* Retrieved May 13, 2021, from Parents: https://www.parents.com/parent-ing/dads/101/bonding-with-baby/

Stevens, H. (2016, February 10). *Key to a satisfying sex life after 5, 10, 20 years? Variety, says study.* Retrieved June 1, 2021, from Chicago Tribune: https://www.chicagotribune.com/columns/heidi-stevens/ct-sex-life-longterm-happiness-balancing-0210-20160210-column.html

Tennyson, A. L. (1850). In Memoriam A. H. H. *Poets.org* .

The Cost of Raising a Child. (2020, February 18). Retrieved March 21, 2021, from US Department of Agriculture: https://www.usda.gov/me-dia/blog/2017/01/13/cost-raising-child

Timmons, J. (2018, January 4). *When Can a Fetus Hear?* Retrieved May 19, 2021, from HealthLine:

https://www.healthline.com/health/pregnancy/when-can-a-fetus-hear

Toub, M. (2021, June 8). *The science of how fatherhood transforms you*. Retrieved May 3, 2021, from Today's Parent: https://www.todaysparent.com/family/parenting/the-science-of-how-fatherhood-transforms-you/

Twenge Ph.D., J. M. (2013, August 12). *How Dare You Say Narcissism Is Increasing?* Retrieved June 5, 2021, from Psychology Today: https://www.psychologytoday.com/us/blog/the-narcissism-epidemic/201308/how-dare-you-say-narcissism-is-increasing

Types of Damaging Fathers and How They Influence Who We Are. (2018, July 10). Retrieved July 3, 2021, from Elisabetta Franzoso: https://www.elisabettafranzoso.com/articles/types-of-damaging-fathers-how-they-influence-who-we-are

Vanalstyne, L. (2016, October 16). *4 Simple Ways to Encourage Dad and Baby Bonding | Mother Rising*. Retrieved May 13, 2021, from Mother Rising: https://www.motherrisingbirth.com/2016/10/dad-and-baby-bonding.html

Vencil, C. (n.d.). *Homemade Baby Food: How I Save $200 a Month Making My Own Baby Food*. Retrieved March 13, 2021, from Caroline Vencil: https://www.carolinevencil.com/homemade-baby-food/

Vermeer, H. J., & van Ijzendoorn, M. H. (2006). Children's elevated cortisol levels at daycare: A review and meta-analysis. *Early Childhood Research Quarterly, 21* (3), 390-401.

Villines, Z. (2021, September 26). *What are the average miscarriage rates by week?* Retrieved June 6, 2021, from Medical News Today: https://www.medicalnewstoday.com/articles/322634

Vinopal, L. (2012, August 30). *Why Fathers Do Not Always Fall Instantly in Love With Their Babies.* Retrieved May 17, 2021, from Fatherly: https://www.fatherly.com/health-science/why-dads-dont-instantly-bond-with-babies/

Wallace, J. B. (2013, July 31). *Help for Overprotective Parents.* Retrieved July 1, 2021, from Real Simple: https://www.realsimple.com/work-life/family/kids-parenting/overprotective-parents

Wallis, L. (2013, March 14). *How it became almost mandatory for dads to attend the birth.* Retrieved April 3, 2021, from BBC News: https://www.bbc.com/news/magazine-21701683?ocid=socialflow_twitter_bbcworld

Weber, L. (2019, May 15). *These extreme athletes are proof that pregnant women don't have to take it easy.* Retrieved May 26, 2021, from The Washington Post: https://www.washingtonpost.-

com/sports/2019/05/15/these-extreme-athletes-are-proof-that-pregnant-women-dont-have-take-it-easy/

WebMD Staff. (n.d.). *Your Guide to Prenatal Testing.* Retrieved June 8, 2021, from Grow by WebMD: https://www.webmd.com/baby/your-guide-prenatal-testing#1

Weismann, C. (2021, October 8). *When Men Don't Feel Sexually Attracted to Their Pregnant Wife.* Retrieved May 26, 2021, from Fatherly: https://www.fatherly.com/love-money/men-not-sexually-attracted-pregnant-wife/

What men REALLY think about sex after birth. (n.d.). Retrieved June 2, 2021, from Mas & Pas: The Parenting Network: https://masandpas.com/what-men-really-think-about-sex-after-birth/

Williams, R. (n.d.). *The decline of fatherhood and the male identity crisis.* Retrieved June 1, 2021, from Father Matters: https://fathermatters.org/the-decline-of-fatherhood-and-the-male-identity-crisis/

Wilson, H. (2017, June 26). *Parental Alienation - 1 in 5 Suffer 'Dad Guilt'.* Retrieved June 1, 2021, from DaddiLife: https://www.daddilife.com/health/wellness/parental-alienation-1-5-suffer-dad-guilt/

Winship, A., & D., L. (1900). *Jukes-Edwards: A Study in Education and Heredity.* R.L. Myers & Co.

NOTES

1. CHILDBIRTH – FOUR VITAL ROLES FOR DADS DURING DELIVERY

1. (20 I Love Lucy Fast Facts)
2. (Rosengren & DeVault)
3. (Odent)
4. (Shapiro)
5. (Clark, 1949)
6. (Wallis, 2013)
7. (Gholipour)

2. CARING FOR A BABY – IT TAKES PRACTICE, NOT INSTINCT

1. (Ghose)
2. (Dhar)
3. (Mayo Clinic)

3. BONDING WITH AN INFANT – BIOLOGICALLY "BUILT FOR THIS"

1. (Livingston & Parker)
2. (Sparrow)
3. (Oxford University)
4. (Nordqvist)
5. (Toub)
6. (Sparrow)
7. (Sparrow)

8. (Vinopal)
9. (Gholipour, 5 Ways Fatherhood Changes a Man's Brain)
10. (Toub)
11. (Timmons)
12. (Vanalstyne)
13. (How Dads Affect Their Newborn Babies)

4. MARITAL STRESS – DON'T BE NAÏVE

1. (Rosen & Kelly)

5. NO SEX – WHO SAID?

1. (Weber)
2. (Pregnancy and Sex Problems)
3. (Weismann)
4. (Barrett, Pendry, Peacock, Victor, Thakar, & Manyonda)
5. (What men REALLY think about sex after birth)
6. (Stevens)

6. WORK-LIFE BALANCE – YOU CAN HAVE ANYTHING, BUT YOU CAN'T HAVE EVERYTHING

1. (Livingston & Parker)
2. (Wilson)
3. (Livingston & Parker)
4. (Wilson)
5. (Kaufman & Petts)
6. (Deanb)

7. IDENTITY LOSS – WHY NEW DADS SHOULD IGNORE 76% OF AMERICANS

1. (Pew Research Center)
2. (Potter)
3. (Williams)
4. (Williams)
5. (Livingston & Parker)

8. CHAOS – "HE POOPED ON THE FLOOR!"

1. (Roosevelt)

9. LOSS OF FREEDOM – NO, IT JUST LOOKS DIFFERENT

1. (Twenge Ph.D.)
2. (DeMonaco)

10. MISCARRIAGE & HEALTH COMPLICATIONS – EVERY REASON FOR HOPE, NOT FEAR

1. (Mayo Clinic)
2. (Villines)
3. (Cleveland Clinic)
4. (Gardner)
5. (Mayo Clinic)
6. (Mayo Clinic)
7. (Cleveland Clinic)
8. (Center for Disease Control and Prevention)

9. (Epidemiology of constipation in North America: a systematic review)
10. (Centers for Disease Control and Prevention)
11. (WebMD Staff)
12. (Mayo Clinic Staff)
13. (Allar)
14. (Tennyson)

11. EVIL, PAIN, AND SUFFERING – IS IT RIGHT TO BRING A CHILD INTO THIS WORLD?

1. (Carlisle)
2. (Johnston & Davey)
3. (Davey)
4. (Djordjevic)
5. (Edmonds)
6. (Eldwin)
7. (Wallace)
8. This quote has been attributed to George Orwell, but it is not clear whether he actually said it: https://quoteinvestigator.com/2013/02/24/truth-revolutionary/

12. FAMILY DYSFUNCTION – BREAKING THE "FIVE-GENERATION RULE"

1. (National Fatherhood Initiative)
2. (Winship & D.)
3. (Schmitt)
4. (Types of Damaging Fathers and How They Influence Who We Are)
5. (Manson)
6. (Manson)

7. (Huerta)

13. FALLING SHORT – HOW NOT TO BE
THE "PERFECT" DAD

1. (Growing Up by Macklemore & Ryan Lewis)
2. (Pew Research Center)
3. (Perfectionism Among Young People Significantly Increased Since 1980s, Study Finds)
4. (Burns)
5. (Bousman)

14. MEDICAL BILLS – HOW TO CUT
COSTS BY 80%

1. (Hatfield)
2. (Hatfield)

15. DAILY EXPENSES – WHAT IT
ACTUALLY COSTS TO RAISE A KID

1. (The Cost of Raising a Child)
2. (Comanor)
3. (Simon)
4. (HOWMUCHISIT.ORG)
5. (Vencil)
6. (Corley)
7. (Dauch, Imwalle, Ocasio, & Metz)
8. (Leake & Robbins)

16. CHILDCARE – DID YOU SAY
$30,000 PER YEAR?

1. (Schochet)
2. (Corcoran, Steinley, & Grady)
3. (Vermeer & van Ijzendoorn)
4. (Ceder)

Made in the USA
Las Vegas, NV
09 October 2022

56882696R00194